Equality

KEY CONCEPTS IN THE SOCIAL SCIENCES

Equality

Stuart White

polity

First published in 2007 by Polity Press

Polity Press
65 Bridge Street
Cambridge CB2 1UR, UK

Polity Press
350 Main Street
Malden, MA 02148, USA

ISBN-10: 0-7456-2773-0
ISBN-13: 978-07456-2773-1
ISBN-10: 0-7456-2774-9 (pb)
ISBN-13: 978-07456-2774-8 (pb)

A catalogue record for this book is available from the British Library.

Typeset in 10.5 on 12 pt Sabon
by SNP Best-set Typesetter Ltd, Hong Kong
Printed and bound in Great Britain by MPG Books Ltd, Bodmin, Cornwall

The publisher has used its best endeavours to ensure that the URLs for external websites referred to in this book are correct and active at the time of going to press. However, the publisher has no responsibility for the websites and can make no guarantee that a site will remain live or that the content is or will remain appropriate.

Every effort has been made to trace all copyright holders, but if any have been inadvertently overlooked the publishers will be pleased to include any necessary credits in any subsequent reprint or edition.

For further information on Polity, visit our website: www.polity.co.uk

Contents

Figures and Tables

Figure

Tables

Acknowledgements

In writing this book I have benefited from discussions with many colleagues over the years. Heartfelt thanks to them all. Additional, particular thanks go to Harry Brighouse and a second, anonymous referee for Polity Press who both read an entire draft of the manuscript and offered excellent comments on how to improve it. Similar thanks go to Ben Saunders, Karl Widerquist and Stephen Winter; and to Nina Wedell who read a full draft of the manuscript and offered valuable advice on its accessibility to a general reader. Louise Knight has been a very patient and supportive editor at Polity Press, ably assisted by Ellen McKinlay, Emma Hutchinson and Helen Gray who kept in touch with me and made encouraging noises in the months and years when I was distracted by other commitments. I am once again, deeply grateful to Katherine Wedell for her love and support throughout the project. I dedicate the book to my parents, Diane and Gordon.

The author and publishers gratefully acknowledge permission to reproduce the following copyright material:

Table 3.1: The class destinations of sons born in 1958 (Britain); reproduced with permissions of Ken Roberts (*Class in Modern Britain*) 2001, p. 197. The table was originally adapted from 'Social Mobility, Individual Ability and the Inheritance of Class Inequality' by Mike Savage and Muriel

Egerton in Sociology 31(4) pp. 645–72 © BSA Publications Ltd, 1997, by permission of Sage Publications Ltd. Table 7.1: Percentage change in Gini coefficient (disposable income, whole population); source Esping-Anderson, 2005, in Giddens and Diamond (eds), 2005, p. 12; reproduced with permission of the author.

For my parents, Diane and Gordon

1
The Demand for Equality

The demand for equality is central to modern politics. It has inspired many of the major political struggles of the past two centuries: the French Revolution, dedicated to the revolutionary trinity of 'liberty, equality, fraternity'; the struggle of Chartists in Britain in the nineteenth century for the right to vote; the movement to abolish slavery in the United States; ideals of fundamental social reconstruction of the kind that motivated the Russian Revolution and, two decades later, the short-lived anarchist uprising in Spain; struggles against fascism and colonialism; the struggle of African-Americans for their civil rights; the emergence of a broad social movement, feminism, dedicated to ending the subordination of women. The demand for equality is, however, both complex and controversial. It is complex in that it is not at base a demand for *a* thing but for a set of things which one might or might not view as necessarily all desirable. It is controversial in that it sometimes seems to threaten other important values.

We get a sense both of the power of the demand for equality, and of why it can seem so controversial, from George Orwell's description of Barcelona in 1936, a city in the middle of a social revolution. In his book, *Homage to Catalonia* (Orwell, 1989 [1938]), Orwell writes as follows:

> when one came straight from England the aspect of Barcelona was something startling and overwhelming. It was the first

time that I had ever been in a town where the working-class was in the saddle. Practically every building of any size had been seized by the workers and was draped with red flags or with the red and black flag of the Anarchists; every wall was scrawled with the hammer and sickle and with the initials of the revolutionary parties; almost every church had been gutted and its images burnt. Churches here and there were being systematically demolished by gangs of workmen. Every shop and cafe had an inscription saying that it had been collectivised; even the bootblacks had been collectivised and their boxes painted red and black. Waiters and shop-walkers looked you in the face and treated you as an equal. Servile and even ceremonial forms of speech had temporarily disappeared. Nobody said '*Senor*' or '*Don*' or even '*Usted*'; everyone called everyone else '*Comrade*' and '*Thou*', and said '*Salud!*' instead of '*Buenos dias*'. Almost my first experience was receiving a lecture from an hotel manager for trying to tip a lift-boy. There were no private motor cars, they had all been commandeered, and all the trams and taxis and much of the other transport were painted red and black. The revolutionary posters were everywhere, flaming from the walls. . . . Down the Ramblas, the wide central artery of the town where crowds of people streamed constantly to and fro, the loudspeakers were bellowing revolutionary songs all day and far into the night. And it was the aspect of the crowds that was the queerest thing of all. In outward appearance it was a town in which the wealthy classes had practically ceased to exist. Except for a small number of women and foreigners there were no 'well-dressed' people at all. Practically everyone wore rough working-class clothes, or blue overalls or some variant of the militia uniform. All this was queer and moving. There was much in it that I did not understand, in some ways I did not even like it, but I recognised it immediately as a state of affairs worth fighting for.

Orwell clearly found many features of this revolutionary society attractive: the way people 'looked you in the face and treated you as an equal'; the sharing out of available wealth and the absence of a rich class showing off to the less fortunate; the sense of fellowship and public-spiritedness associated with this state of affairs. Yet Orwell confesses that 'in some ways I did not even like it', and one can sympathize with this ambivalence. What about the people in Barcelona who still wanted to go to those demolished churches? Do we

feel comfortable with the image of a society in which everyone feels obliged to paint everything red and black and walk
around in 'blue overalls' or a 'militia uniform'? Do we want
political propaganda – even propaganda promoting equality
– blaring out all day from public loudspeakers? In some ways,
Orwell's picture of revolutionary Barcelona anticipates the
picture of a totalitarian society which he explores in his later
work, *Nineteen Eighty-Four* (Orwell, 2004 [1949]). Is the
price of equality necessarily the loss of liberty and the cowing
of people into a state of scared uniformity? The aim of this
book is to unpack the complexity of the demand for equality; to clarify what motivates it; and, in the process, to explore
some of the anxieties about liberty and other values that this
demand provokes.

Two restrictions of the discussion should be noted. First, I
assume throughout that we are talking about equality as a
demand that applies to the organization of relationships
between human beings. I shall not consider how far or in
what ways the demand for equality ought to apply to relationships between human and non-human animals. Second,
I assume throughout that our concern is with human beings
who are living at the same point in time. I shall not consider
how the value of equality might inform our consideration of
relationships between human beings living at different points
in time, for example, between those of us alive today and
those living, say, two hundred years hence. This is not
because I think equality has no place in thinking about our
relationships with non-human animals, or across multiple
generations, or that the value is not very important in these
contexts. Peter Singer and other philosophers have made a
very strong case that the interests of non-human animals
should count equally with those of humans (Singer, 1990
[1975]). And respect for the moral equality of human beings
may well have important implications in thinking about how
members of one generation should behave towards the environment (Wissenburg, 1998; Barry, 1999). But every book
has to draw a limit somewhere in order to keep the discussion within manageable bounds, and these are topics that I
have chosen to bracket here. Hopefully, while I do not discuss
these issues directly, the reader will find my discussion of
equality in other contexts useful in approaching them.

This chapter carries out some groundwork for the rest of the book. We begin, in section 1.1, by distinguishing different forms of equality. We will then consider, in section 1.2, the different ways in which one might think that these kinds of equality are valuable.

1.1   Forms of equality

As said, the demand for equality is not a demand for a thing, but a demand for many things, and people can and do disagree about the relative worth of these different things. As a preliminary step in clarifying the complexity of equality we may distinguish five different categories of equality all of which enter, in more or less controversial ways, into the demand for equality in modern politics.

1. *Legal equality.* In any large-scale society, effective and fair social cooperation seems to require that social relations be shaped and constrained by laws: general rules which people can be punished for trangressing. The state is the institution, or set of institutions, which defines these laws (legislative function), seeks to apply and enforce them (executive function), and to provide fair ways of assessing whether people have trangressed them and determining punishment (judicial function). Let us say that someone who is bound by the law of a given state is a *subject* of this state. Legal equality requires, first, that if any member of society is a subject, then all are. The status of being a subject should be universal amongst members of the state. No person should be, as we say, 'above the law'. Historically, it has also been considered important that the law itself does not define different classes of subject, some of whom have rights or privileges denied to others: the law should be the same for all, the status of being a subject essentially uniform in content. (We will see in chapter 6 that this requirement is in fact somewhat controversial.) In addition, the law should be applied (and be seen to be applied) in an impartial, unbiased way. Thus, if penalties are being handed down for a particular crime, the penalties should be relevantly similar regardless of people's class, gender or ethnicity. This is the idea captured in famil-

iar sayings such as that there should not be 'one law for the poor and another for the rich'. Further, the state should provide protection for its members on a relevantly equal basis. The poor, for example, should not enjoy less police protection than the rich, merely because they are poor. Each citizen's interests should be given the same value in the allocation of the state's protective and judicial resources.

2. *Political equality.* Equality under the law does not necessarily entail equality in the process of making the law. This is where the demand for political equality comes in. The core idea is that those who are subject to the commands of a state should have equal right to participate in formulating the laws on which these commands are based. It seems necessary to qualify this claim to some extent; since meaningful participation requires at least some minimum level of intellectual development, many think it justifiable to exclude children and those with severe learning disabilities from equal political rights (though it is possible to enfranchise even these groups by proxy; see Van Parijs, 1998). Here, the relevant political rights most obviously include the right to vote and the right to stand for political office. If the point of these rights is to give people real control over lawmaking, however, and to ensure that lawmaking is based on informed reflection, then it is vital that citizens also have rights of freedom of association and freedom of expression. These freedoms are crucial in enabling citizens to get their grievances and ideals on to the political agenda and to think about an issue in an informed way before they exercise their rights to vote (Dahl, 1998, pp. 37–8).

In thinking about political equality it is important to distinguish between formal and effective political rights. A destitute person might have the same political rights in law as a very rich person. But the difference in their economic positions can clearly make a difference to their effective ability to exercise these rights. The rich person might be able to buy up a large amount of advertising time on TV to campaign for a preferred law or candidate, while a very poor person might not be able to spare the time from work even to vote. In a private-property, market-based economy, richer individuals will have a lot of control over business investment decisions and this power might constrain how government can act. For these reasons, supporters of political equality often argue that if political equality is to be real and not a sham it is important to consider how the distribution of income and wealth affects citizens' effective abilities to exercise their political rights. To prevent economic inequality undermining the substance of political equality it may be necessary to limit economic inequality directly and/or to control the ways in which economic advantage can translate into political influence. However, proposed measures, such as placing restrictions on private campaign spending and establishing popular control over business investment decisions, raise strong opposition on the grounds that they will interfere with important personal liberties.

   3. *Social equality.*   I use the term social equality here to refer to two ideas that feature in the modern demand for equality. The first is the idea of *status equality.* By status here we mean, as David Miller puts it, 'a person's basic standing within a society, as manifested by the way in which he or she is regarded by the public institutions and by other individuals' (Miller, 1994, p. 206). In a society with status inequality, there is a widely shared sense that some people occupy a superior station in life to others due to their family and social class or their gender or their ethnicity. Such a society is one in which some feel they can look down on others and others feel they have to be deferential to people higher up the status hierarchy. It may also be a society in which people do not feel comfortable mixing with people above or below them in the social scale except on very regulated and predictable terms. In the city of Oxford in the 1930s the local town council erected some walls for no purpose other than to separate a working-class estate of council housing from a middle-class, private housing development. This reflects the kind of social separation that can occur in a society in which many people have attitudes of the kind we associate with status inequality. The 'Cutteslowe Walls', eventually pulled down in the 1950s, became a byword in Britain for class snobbery and resentment (Mabey, 1966, p. 7). A society based on status equality is one in which people's relationships are uncluttered by attitudes like snobbery and deference. It is a society 'in which people deal with one another simply as individuals,

taking account only of personal capacities, needs, achievements, etc., without the blocking effect of status differences' (Miller, 1994, p. 207). Orwell's description of revolutionary Barcelona gives us a sense of what can happen when a society suddenly springs out of traditional status inequalities: 'Waiters and shop-walkers looked you in the face and treated you as an equal. Servile and even ceremonial forms of speech had temporarily disappeared.'

The second idea which might be referred to as a form of social equality is the *absence of domination* in people's everyday social relationships. By domination here I mean a situation in which one person is in a position of power to dictate to another (Pettit, 1997; Skinner, 1998). This power can be granted by the state, as in traditional marital law which gave husbands considerable power over their wives (Mill, 1989 [1869]). But such power might also arise in other ways. The employer might have power to dominate the life of the worker because the worker lacks an alternative source of employment and subsistence. The husband might be able to dominate his wife because she relies on him for a roof over her head. A 'society of equals' (Scheffler, 2003) is, in part, a society in which people have a high degree of security against such domination. Put crudely, it is a society in which everyone has the effective freedom to tell any other person to get lost.

4. *Economic equality.* The modern politics of equality has focused a great deal on the demand for some kind of economic equality. The Industrial Revolution of the nineteenth century initially generated severe contrasts in income and wealth which, in turn, stimulated a wave of imaginative thinking about how society might be restructured to prevent gross economic inequality. This produced the various currents of socialist thought which exerted a huge influence over politics in the twentieth century, and which still retain some influence today.

Looking back at the ferment of ideas at this time, we can roughly distinguish at least four basic views about what the demand for equality in the economic sphere consists in. The first is what we would today call *meritocracy*, which we will discuss in depth in chapter 3. In feudal societies, one's social position is typically inherited. If one is born into the wrong social class, then one has very little opportunity to rise to leading positions in society. The founding of the American republic, together with the French Revolution, challenged traditional conceptions of society as a stable class hierarchy with the idea of the 'career open to talents'. To some extent, the spirit of meritocracy was in keeping with the new industrial capitalism. But does a child growing up in desperate poverty, as so many did at this time, really have the same chance to rise as a child growing up in affluence? Circumstances prompted serious reflection on the underlying structures of ownership and other determinants of income distribution in the new economy.

This brings us to the second view which was influential at this time, which we may term *land egalitarianism*. The opening proposition is that the earth – land and other natural resources – is in some significant sense the common property of society. In the first edition of his *Social Statics* (1872 [1850]), the leading Victorian philosopher Herbert Spencer argued that:

> Equity . . . does not permit [private] property in land . . . the assumption that land can be held as [private] property, involves that the whole globe may become the private domain of a part of its inhabitants; and if, by consequence, the rest of its inhabitants can then exercise their faculties – can then exist even – only by the consent of the landowners; it is manifest, that an exclusive possession of the soil necessitates an infringement of the law of equal freedom. For, men who cannot 'live and move and have their being' without the leave of others, cannot be equally free with those others. (p. 132)

If the land is divided up for individual use, then this must be done on terms that acknowledge each individual's claim, as an equal, to a share of this asset. Spencer's proposal is that the land should be owned by the state and rented out to individuals to use for a commercial rent: 'Instead of leasing his acres from an isolated proprietor, the farmer would lease them from the nation. . . . Under [this system] all men would be equally landlords' (Spencer, 1872 [1850], p. 141). The rental income would return to the community as a whole.

Henry George argued in similar terms in his hugely influential *Progress and Poverty* (1966 [1879]) for a tax on the site value of land as a way of recouping for all members of society their rightful claim to a share of the earth. A third view, which incorporates and goes beyond land egalitarianism, is what we may term – alas, rather clumsily – *means of production egalitarianism*. (By 'means of production' we mean land *plus* other things like factories and technologies.) Karl Marx and Friedrich Engels argued that capitalism was dividing society into two 'hostile camps': the bourgeoisie, owners of the means of production, and the proletariat, owning no means of production and thus forced to live by the sale of their labour-power to the bourgeoisie (Marx and Engels, 2002 [1848], Marx, 1990 [1864]). Moreover, in time, capitalism would press the living standards of the proletariat down to extreme poverty. The solution was to expropriate the bourgeoisie: to take the means of production into the common ownership of society. The share of the social product that previously went to the bourgeoisie, as rent, interest and profit on the use of land and capital – in Marx's terms, 'surplus value' – could then be harvested (or reinvested) for the benefit of all. In essence, the idea was to make all citizens akin to shareholders in society's land and capital, each with a roughly equal stake.

Once the bourgeoisie has been expropriated, however, how should workers themselves be paid? Some socialists argued that society should pay workers according to the value that their work contributes to society. Others disagreed. While accepting an initial role for this principle in the early stages of socialism, Marx argued strongly against adopting this as the ultimate goal:

> But one man is superior to another physically or mentally and so supplies more labour in the same time, or can labour for a longer time. . . . Further, one worker is married, another not; one man has more children than another, and so on and so forth. . . . In a higher phase of communist society . . . then can the narrow horizon of bourgeois right be crossed in its entirety and society inscribe on its banners: from each according to his ability, to each according to his needs! (Marx, 1875, in McLellan (ed.) 1977, pp. 568–9)

We might term this, our fourth view, *communism*. On this view, the higher output of workers with greater productive power ought not to revert to the individual workers but should be shared out within the community on the basis of need. In effect, then, the talents of the skilled workers also become a kind of commonly owned resource. Talented workers are drawn to deploy their talents, either by a sense of duty or (as in fact Marx suggests) by intrinsic attraction to suitable work, and the resulting product becomes part of the common pool. Marx was by no means alone or even that original in holding such a position. The slogan he refers to in the above passage was already widely adopted by socialists in the 1840s. On the anarchist wing of the socialist movement, Kropotkin endorsed the principle (Kropotkin, 1970 [1913]). Of course, the principle provokes a number of questions. On what basis is society to assess differences in needs? Does neediness have a claim to satisfaction independently of how the person came to be needy (for instance, do people have a less valid claim to assistance if they are responsible for adding to their neediness)? Does distribution according to need not require some qualification to provide workers with incentives to develop their skills and work hard?

We need not go further into the differences between these four views here. For now it is enough to see just how central the concern for appropriate economic equality has been in the politics of the past two centuries, and to see how this concern has motivated quite a range of programmes for the reform of society's basic economic arrangements. We will consider the underlying philosophical issues in later chapters (see especially chapters 3, 4 and 5).

5. *Moral equality.* The demands for legal, political, social and economic equality are demands for certain kinds of social arrangements. They are intended to guide the design of major social institutions. Distinct from these institutional demands, as we might thus call them, and possibly motivating them, is a principle of moral equality.

Assume that we are talking about the members of a specific nation-state. The principle of moral equality says that each member of the state has equal worth. Accordingly, it holds that in designing society's basic institutions, we ought to treat each member's interests – their morally significant interests in things such as freedoms, resources and so on – as placing equally pressing claims on how our society is organized. My interests, in the indicated sense, count as much as yours. This does not necessarily mean that society has to be designed to secure equal satisfaction of these interests. But it does put the burden of justification on the supporter of inequality. There need to be good reasons for inequality in the legal, political, social and economic domains, reasons that are consistent with affirming the equal worth of each member of the community. Ronald Dworkin has expressed this idea by saying that there is a duty on the state (that is, on *us* as citizens who, in a democracy, are responsible for the laws of the state) to arrange social institutions in a way that expresses *equal concern and respect* for each member of the community:

> Can we turn our backs on equality? No government is legitimate that does not show equal concern and respect for the fate of all those citizens over whom it claims dominion and from whom it claims allegiance. Equal concern is the sovereign virtue of the political community – without it government is only tyranny – and when a nation's wealth is very unequally distributed, as the wealth of even very prosperous nations now is, then its equal concern is suspect. For the distribution of wealth is the product of a legal order: a citizen's wealth massively depends on which laws his community has enacted. . . . When the government enacts or sustains one set of such laws rather than another, it is not only predictable that some citizens' lives will be worsened by its choice but also, to a considerable degree, which citizens these will be. In the prosperous democracies it is predictable, whenever government curtails welfare programs or declines to expand them, that its decision will keep the lives of poor people bleak. We must be prepared to explain, to those who suffer in that way, why they have nevertheless been treated with the equal concern that is their right. (Dworkin, 2000, pp. 1–2)

Note how Dworkin here ties the principle of moral equality to the justification of state authority: the authority of the state is legitimate only to the extent that it enacts and sustains a social system that is reasonably defensible in terms of this principle. This implies that the scope of the principle stretches as far as the political community. But what about people outside this community (assuming there are such people, i.e., we are not in a world state)? If people as such have equal worth, then should we not seek to apply the principle globally, to the whole of humanity? Is equality a specifically political virtue, one that comes into play only among people who are bound to obey the same political authority? Or is it a pre-political virtue that applies between human beings as such, even between human beings who perhaps have no interaction with each other, let alone common membership of a given state?

Some argue that we should not, or at least need not, make this move (Miller, 1998; Nagel, 2005). They do not deny that we have important obligations to all human beings as such. No human being should be vulnerable to torture, arbitrary arrest or starvation. All human beings have certain basic rights related to these interests, and we all share in some degree in the obligation to see that these rights are respected. (For example, if an ethnic minority in another nation is being persecuted, then my nation and your nation may have an obligation to admit members of this minority as asylum seekers.) But these thinkers do deny that the concern for distributive equality, for regulating relative differences in goods like income and wealth, applies across nations. If people in nation X are much richer on average than people in nation Y, but people in nation Y are not starving or otherwise suffering intense deprivation, then people in nation X need not worry about the relative difference in income and wealth. But others, so-called cosmopolitan egalitarians, think it clear that we should care about such differences. Intermediate positions, which see the concern for distributive equality as probably confined to people who share membership of a state, but which allow for obligations to others well beyond a very basic 'moral minimum', are also conceivable (Cohen and Sabel, 2006). In the bulk of the discussion that follows I shall assume that we are considering the demand for equality in the context of people who belong to the same nation-state, but in the book's final chapter we will explore further the debate around cosmopolitan egalitarianism.

The discussion above draws our attention to an important distinction between egalitarian and humanitarian concerns.

Consider the demand: 'Nobody should be hungry'. While the effort to end hunger for all might well reduce relative differences in income (as we tax the rich to feed the poor), the motivation is not to reduce relative incomes difference for its own sake but to ensure that nobody is hungry. The underlying, fundamental concern is with people being *badly off*, not with their being *less well off*. In Joseph Raz's terms, the demand to end hunger is a 'satiable' demand, one that 'can be completely met' (Raz, 1986, p. 235). While we can talk of one person being hungrier than another, at some point the lessening of hunger turns into the absence of hunger and the demand to end hunger is met. If two people are at this point, it makes no sense to go on and ask whether one of them has more of this good, the absence of hunger, than the other. We just say that neither is hungry. Raz contrasts a political programme which consists entirely of various humanitarian demands of this satiable kind ('nobody should be hungry', 'nobody should be homeless', etc.) with what he calls a 'strict egalitarian' programme which is focused on relative differences in goods (income, wealth, pleasure) for its own sake. Humanitarianism and egalitarianism are not the same thing (though, of course, they are not exclusive of one another insofar as an egalitarian can support humanitarian demands).

However, while the contrast that Raz draws is substantially correct, there do seem to be some satiable demands that we can and should describe as egalitarian (albeit not as 'strict egalitarian' in Raz's sense). In particular, consider the idea of social equality as the absence of domination in everyday social relationships. This seems to be a satiable demand. While we can talk of one person being less dominated than another, at some point the lessening of domination turns into the absence of domination and the demand to end domination is met. If two people are at this point, it makes no sense to go on and ask whether one of them has more of this good, the absence of domination, than the other. We just say that neither suffers domination. But in this case, it seems perfectly right to describe the satiable demand for the absence of domination as an egalitarian concern. The absence of domination in everyday social relationships clearly is central to the notion of a 'society of equals' ('no masters, no slaves'). What I think this shows is that our equality talk combines two related, but distinct, sorts of idea. On the one hand, it includes essentially distributive concerns about the relative amounts of certain goods that people have (Raz's 'strict egalitarianism'). On the other, it includes concerns about the sort of relationships that people have to one another. We want equality (or less inequality) in the distribution of goods, *and* we want people to relate 'as equals' (for related discussions, see Miller, 2000a, pp. 230–3; Scheffler, 2003). How these two kinds of equality demand are best integrated into an overall conception of equality is a very complex and demanding question. We will encounter some of the debates surrounding this question in the course of this book.

1.2   Forms of value

We have taken a preliminary look at the content of the demand for equality. This has already revealed just how complex, and controversial in its complexity, the demand is. But why do we want equality? Why, and in what way(s), is it a good thing, a value that should inform political action? We will explore these questions more fully in later chapters, but again it will help to lay out some preliminary thoughts here.

First, a given kind of equality might have *instrumental value*: value derived from the way in which it serves to promote some other value (Clayton and Williams, 2000, pp. 4–5, drawing on Raz, 1986, p. 177).[1] Take the case of economic equality. Many arguments for increasing economic equality focus on how it allegedly advances some other good. For instance, someone might argue for increasing economic equality because it improves the position of the poor. Their concern here is not with equality as such, but with how greater equality serves the value of ensuring everyone a decent standard of life. The fundamental value is ensuring all a decent standard of life (Scanlon, 2003, pp. 203–4). Or someone might think that it is intrinsically good for a society to enjoy a spirit of community and fellowship, and desire a degree of economic equality as a means to this end. If the amount of happiness or 'utility' derived from a unit of income decreases as we move up the income scale then more equal divisions of available income should give us more happiness in total: the rich will lose less happiness from losing a unit of income than the poor gain from receiving this income (see Bentham, 1973 [1823], p. 200). For this reason, moves towards greater economic equality might increase total happiness, and historically many supporters of greater economic equality have defended such moves on this instrumental ground (see Jackson, 2004, for discussion of one such group of thinkers).

Sometimes an instrumental argument for economic equality might focus on the way this promotes some other kind of equality. For example, as already intimated, some argue that a high degree of economic equality is necessary to make political equality real and not a sham. One might similarly argue that a degree of economic equality is necessary to preserve status equality. If there are large inequalities of income and wealth, then this might create a culture in which the rich look down their noses at the poor, while the poor come to see the rich as a separate class of 'natural' superiors. Again, economic equality might be valued because it is seen as instrumental to the other aspect of social equality noted above, the absence of domination in everyday social relationships. Where there are great economic inequalities, some people may become so reliant on others for their basic well-being that it is easy for the well off to dictate to them and control their lives: 'Are you going to church, Jones? If not, I may have to ask you to seek employment elsewhere . . .' (see Scanlon, 2003, for further discussion of these links between economic and other kinds of equality).

Instrumental arguments are not confined to economic equality. One can argue, for example, that political equality is valuable, in part, because of the way it promotes status equality. In a society that practises 'one person one vote', political processes help to affirm the equal status of each person as a member of the community. On the other hand, the denial of the vote to a group of people is a very public expression that this group has lower status in the community. It demeans and degrades, and hence undermines status equality (see chapter 2). One might also argue (though this is much more questionable) that political equality serves economic equality. Certainly, one of the main reasons why propertied classes historically have opposed democracy is a fear that the lower classes will use their political rights to redistribute property from the rich to themselves (see the discussion of the Putney Debates in chapter 2), though in practice this fear seems not to have been borne out to anything like the feared extent.

In short, legal, political, social and economic equality might all be valued instrumentally in view of how they promote other values, including other kinds of equality. Although each specific instrumental connection is one that needs research to be confirmed, there are good reasons for thinking that each of these types of equality has instrumental value in one or more respects.

Second, we might value a given kind of equality because we think that it is, in itself, *inherently fair or just*. For instance, we might view some degree of economic equality as desirable not because, or not only because, it promotes political equality, or community, or the greatest sum of human happiness, but because we think it is in itself right and fair. To see the nature of this sort of claim it may help to step back for a moment and consider in a general way the relationship between fairness and justice on the one hand and equality on the other.

Just about every notion of justice or fairness seems to employ one elementary notion of equality, that of 'treating like cases alike'. For example, if we have a rule stating that 'Good X should be allocated according to how far people have characteristic Y', then justice requires that people with equal Y should get equal X; it would be unjust to give people with equal Ys unequal Xs as this is not treating like cases alike. Or say we are playing a game of soccer and the referee makes biased decisions against one team. He sends a player from the United States team off the field for a foul, but does not do the same for a player from England who commits a similar foul. Again, the referee is failing to treat like cases alike and this dissimilarity of treatment is unjust. Being just in this sense, which is essentially a matter of consistency in the application of rules, is sometimes called formal justice: 'If we think of justice as always expressing a kind of equality, then formal justice requires that in their administration laws and institutions should apply equally (that is, in the same way) to those belonging to the classes defined by them' (Rawls, 1999a, p. 51).

However, formal justice, or 'justice as regularity' as it is also called (Rawls, 1999a, p. 207), need not entail substantive justice. To see the difference, let us fill out the formula given above: 'Good X should be allocated according to how far people have characteristic Y.' Imagine that X is wealth and Y is, say, height. So the rule says that we should distribute wealth in society according to how tall people are: tall people are to get more wealth simply because they are tall. Now a society might be absolutely scrupulous in how it applies this rule, ensuring that there is a perfect proportion between wealth and height. But would such a society be just? Surely not. For even though the rule itself is applied justly, the rule's content is unjust. Why on earth should tall people be advantaged relative to shorter people in the way the rule prescribes? The principle of moral equality, that all citizens are owed equal concern and respect, does not necessarily imply that everybody in our society ought to get exactly the same amount of every good, but it does require that we be able to advance good reasons for any differentiation we allow, and differentiation on the basis of height seems entirely arbitrary. It is on a par with saying that some people should get more wealth than others because they have, say, lighter skins; and as Bernard Williams puts it:

> The principle that men should be differentially treated in respect of their welfare merely on grounds of their colour is not a special sort of moral principle, but (if anything) a purely arbitrary assertion of will, like that of some Caligulan ruler who decided to execute everyone whose names contained three 'R's. (Williams, 1973, p. 233)[2]

Thus, while the principle of moral equality demands formal justice, it also seems to set some limits on what we can reasonably view as substantively just. Many rules that we might use to regulate the distribution of income and wealth in our society are reasonably considered to be substantively unjust because, even when applied perfectly consistently, they put some people at an entirely arbitrary disadvantage compared with others. The notion of intrinsic justice, rooted in the principle of moral equality, enters in this way into arguments for other kinds of equality, as we shall see in the chapters that follow.

Some political theorists, however, have cautioned us against interpreting all demands for equality as demands for justice. In particular, David Miller has argued forcefully that status equality should be seen as a value that is 'free-standing and independent of justice' (Miller, 2000a, p. 239). Miller distinguishes the idea of status equality from what he calls 'distributive' conceptions of equality. The latter specify 'that benefits of a certain kind – rights, for instance – should be distributed equally, because justice requires this' (Miller, 2000a, pp. 231–2). But the idea of status equality:

> is not in this sense distributive. It does not specify directly any distribution of rights or resources. Instead, it identifies a social ideal, the ideal of a society in which people regard and treat one another as equals – in other words, a society that does not place people in hierarchically ranked categories such as classes. (p. 232)

When we object to status inequality, Miller argues, we are not protesting the unjust distribution of some good, but: 'we are objecting to social relationships that we find unseemly – they involve incomprehension and mistrust between rich and poor, for instance, or arrogance on one side and obeisance on the other' (p. 232).

I am not convinced by Miller's argument that status equality is a value that is 'free-standing and independent of justice'. Let's consider an example. Take the case of African-Americans in the 1950s. The position of African-Americans at this time had the three following features: many African-Americans lacked effective civil and political rights; many African-Americans suffered unjust economic disadvantage; and African-Americans occupied one of the lower rungs of the United States's status hierarchy. Many whites viewed them as inferior and wanted to be physically separate from them. Moreover, it is conceivable that some African-Americans internalized these attitudes and lived with a sense of inferiority. In his moving essay, 'Down at the Cross', James

Baldwin wrote about the experience of status inequality as follows:

> Negroes in this country – and Negroes do not, strictly or legally speaking, exist in any other – are taught really to despise themselves from the moment their eyes open on the world. This world is white and they are black. White people hold the power, which means that they are superior to blacks (intrinsically that is: God decreed it so), and the world has innumerable ways of making this difference known and felt and feared. Long before the Negro child perceives this difference, and even longer before he understands it, he has begun to react to it, he has begun to be controlled by it. (Baldwin, 1985 [1962], pp. 39–40).

Now, returning to Miller's argument, it seems perfectly intelligible to say that African-Americans at the time we are considering suffered injustice; one aspect of this being precisely that they were towards the bottom of a status hierarchy in the way that Baldwin so vividly describes. It also seems perfectly intelligible to say that in order to become more just, American society had to overcome this status inequality. But if these propositions are intelligible, then it seems perfectly plausible to think that when we protest status inequality we are protesting it because it is a kind of injustice. Baldwin's essay suggests one reason why status inequality is unjust: it works against the victim's sense of self-worth and self-confidence and, in this way, can discourage the individual from thinking creatively and imaginatively about what he or she wants to do with his or her life. The low-status individual is 'controlled' by the perceptions of the high-status other. He or she becomes fearfully concerned, as we put it, to know his or her place. Such attitudes can inhibit a person's ability to live well as much as a lack of civil and political rights or a lack of economic resources. The philosopher John Rawls captures this idea when he argues that one of the things that just institutions must secure is the 'social bases of self-respect' (Rawls, 1999a, p. 386): 'Without [self-respect] nothing may seem worth doing, or if some things have value for us, we lack the will to strive for them. All desire and activity becomes empty and vain, and we sink into apathy and cynicism.'[3] We now have good evidence that assignment to low social status damages health, not only through the impact that status can have on income and wealth but due to the psychological effects of being branded as a social inferior.[4]

Those who claim that equality is intrinisically just and desirable, in the distributive sense we distinguished towards the end of section 1.1, face another important challenge: the levelling-down objection (Parfit, 2000, pp. 97–9; see also Raz, 1986, pp. 227, 234–5). Consider table 1.1. The table describes three hypothetical worlds. Each gives different levels of overall life-opportunity to the members of two social classes, classes A and B. Imagine that the laws we have currently put us in world X. Starting in X, a shift to Y involves levelling-down: we increase equality, but no person is actually made better off by this and some people are made worse off. For example, we might imagine that in world X, half the population (class B) is blind, while the rest is fully sighted; in world Y everyone is blind (an example inspired by Temkin, 2000, pp. 126–61). Now, if we had to choose between X and Y, which system should we choose? Many people regard it as obvious that we should choose X over Y. Of course, Y is more equal than X. But then, so the argument runs, this just goes to show how silly it is to care about equality as such. To care about equality as such, and to argue on the basis of equality's intrinsic justice for Y over X, allegedly makes no moral sense given that the option of equality *makes nobody better off and makes some people worse off.* Note that a shift from X to Z, were world Z also a possibility, is not vulnerable to this objection. While the people in class A lose out from this shift, the shift to Z does make some people, those in class B, somewhat better off. (Perhaps scientists have found a way to give the people in class B a little bit of sight by putting a chemical in the atmosphere, but the chemical also gives nasty stomach cramps to people who are fully sighted.) So this is not a case of levelling-down.

Table 1.1   Levelling-down: three possible worlds

	World X	World Y	World Z
Class A	20	10	12
Class B	10	10	11

The levelling-down objection certainly shows us that when we come to consider what we want in our world, equality is not the *only* or the *supreme* value at stake. There are a number of values that we have and we understandably want to take them all into account in thinking about the sort of world we want and what action we should take to make the world a better place. In this case, a single-minded insistence on equality conflicts with efficiency, the idea that a state of affairs is better than another if at least one person is better off in it and no one is worse off. Most of us think that in a case like that just described we should give priority to efficiency over equality.

However, from the fact that equality is not the only or the supreme value it does not follow that equality is not itself intrinsically just and valuable for this reason. Having presented a case like that just described, Larry Temkin comments:

> the anti-egalitarian will incredulously ask, do I really think there is some respect in which a world where only some are blind [world X] is worse than one where all are [world Y]? Yes. Does this mean I think it would be better if we blinded everyone? No. Equality is not all that matters. But it matters some. (Temkin, 2000, p. 155)

Stated as boldly as this, Temkin's comment might seem a little strange, so let me elaborate what he is getting at. If we choose X over Y, then we opt for a world in which some people are worse off than others through no fault of their own. This inequality is, in and of itself, unjust. It is unjust for some people to be better off than others due to accidents of birth. Thus, world Y would be better than X *in one specific way*, namely, that it would contain none of this unjust inequality. But in saying this we do not have to take the further step of claiming that equality is the only value we should care about or that it always takes precedence over other values. Recognizing that there is a plurality of ultimate values, and that they sometimes tragically conflict, we can also say that, in such a case, the claims of equality must give way to the claims of another important value.

Note that when we accept that another value has priority over equality in a given case, this is not necessarily a question of justice, as represented by an equality demand, being trumped by some consideration *external* to justice; for it might be that the considerations that trump equality in a given case are *also* considerations of justice.

To see this, consider the potential conflict, noted at the start of this chapter, between demands for equality and demands for personal liberty. Imagine we have to choose between a world in which there is great economic equality and very limited freedom of speech and a world in which there is full freedom of speech and much less economic equality. One might reasonably think that each world is more inherently just than the other in one important respect: one is more just by virtue of its greater economic equality; the other by virtue of its respect for freedom of speech. In such a case, we have to balance two competing claims of justice, deciding which has priority. I cannot review all the arguments here, but some would argue that in such a case justice requires that we give priority to freedom of speech: on balance, all things considered, the world with free speech and greater economic inequality is the just (or, at least, more just) world. The conflict between equality and efficiency, to which the levelling-down objection points, can also be seen as a conflict between competing considerations of justice. For it is plausible to say that just treatment of our fellow citizens requires that we give at least some weight to the principle of efficiency, as defined above, in determining how we live.

Having reflected on the levelling-down objection, we may now usefully distinguish three respects in which specific types of equality might be said to be valuable:

1. *Instrumental value.* First, we might see a given type of equality as instrumentally valuable because of the way it serves some other value, including other types of equality.
2. *Intrinsically just.* Second, we might regard a given type of equality as valuable because it is intrinsically just, where our understanding of what is substantively just is shaped by the underlying principle of moral equality.
3. *Supreme value.* Third, we might see equality as intrinsically just and, for this reason (or possibly for some other reason), as the supreme value.

The levelling-down objection shows how implausible it is to maintain that equality is the supreme value. It requires us to reject the position, called *pure egalitarianism* by Derek Parfit, which holds the claims of equality should always prevail (Parfit, 2000, p. 84). But, as Temkin suggests, one can acknowledge the force of the levelling-down objection and remain what Parfit calls a *pluralist egalitarian* (pp. 84–5). As a pluralist egalitarian one might think that equality is intrinsically just. But one accepts that this claim of justice can conflict with other values, including other claims of justice, and that when it does the claims of other values should sometimes, and to some extent, prevail.

Pluralist egalitarianism must be distinguished from what Parfit calls 'the priority view'. This holds that we should judge states of the world in terms of how well off the worst off are in them. The difference between the two views is subtle but real. Go back to the choice between X and Y. Even if the pluralist egalitarian thinks we should choose X over Y, she still thinks there is a respect in which Y is better than X, namely, that it is more equal. The priority view, by contrast, does not commit us to seeing Y as better than X in any respect. On the priority view, we do not assess states of the world in terms of equality as such, but only in terms of how well off the worst off are. Since the worst off are no better off under Y than under X, the priority view gives us no reason to see Y as better than X in any way.[5] In practice, the two positions may not be far apart. If the pluralist egalitarian gives a strong weight to the value of efficiency, as defined above, then her policy prescriptions will tend to converge with those of the priority view. But, for the reason just explained, the pluralist egalitarian will prefer X to Y with a heavier heart. Given the arbitrary inequality between people in world X, I think, with Temkin, that we ought to have a somewhat heavy heart when we prefer X to Y. Thus, at base, my intuitions are pluralist egalitarian rather than those of the priority view. The reader should reflect on her own intuitions.

Having discussed the content of the demand for equality, and the ways in which equality demands emerge as values to guide our thinking, I conclude with a brief overview of the rest of the book. In chapter 2 we will consider in more depth the nature of, and justification for, the demand for political equality. Chapters 3, 4 and 5 then examine the content of, and justification for, the demand for economic equality. Chapters 3 and 4 in effect explore what kind and level of economic equality is intrinsically just, while chapter 5 returns us to the potential conflict between equality and efficiency. The relationship between economic equality and social and political equality is also considered. In chapter 6, we explore the argument that an insistence on strict legal equality, in the sense of uniform rights and duties for all citizens, might in fact work against the deeper requirements of showing citizens equal concern and respect. Chapter 7 examines how (if at all) the demand for equality is likely to feature in future politics. This chapter includes a fuller discussion of whether and in what sense the demand for equality (specifically, economic equality) should be seen as having global, rather than merely national, scope. Throughout the book, we will identify and grapple with one of the central controversies of modern politics: how far the demands for equality and liberty conflict.

2
Democracy

For really I think that the poorest he that is in England has a life to live as the greatest he; and therefore truly, sir, I think it's clear that every man that is to live under a government ought first by his own consent to put himself under that government; and I do think that the poorest man in England is not at all bound in a strict sense to that government that he has not had a voice to put himself under.

Thomas Rainborough, 1647,
quoted in Andrew Sharp, *The English Levellers*

All modern political systems are systems of command: people within them have the power to issue binding commands in the name of the state and to issue further commands to punish those who disobey. Commands might include rules about taxation, traffic, religious worship, expression of ideas, participation in armed conflict and so on. A key question for political philosophy is: How should a society distribute the power to author such commands amongst its members? One possible answer is: this power should be distributed equally amongst the citizens. This is political equality. It is equality with respect to the power to author binding commands on the subjects of the state. Democratic political systems are based on this principle of political equality. This is reflected in their commitment to the idea of 'one person, one vote', and to equal rights of political participation in a context of freedom of expression and association. These days, we tend to take the value of democracy, and thus of political equality, as a given. It seems obviously the right thing. Historically, however, democracy has been very much the exception as a political system. Moreover, at the philosophical level, many of the canonical thinkers of Western political thought have been very sceptical of its value.

In this chapter we will explore the rise and defensibility of the democratic ideal. Section 2.1 outlines the classical doctrines of natural aristocracy and of the mixed constitution, ideas that we can trace back to Plato and Aristotle. In section 2.2 we then look at the emergence of social contract theories of legitimate authority in the early modern period and at their complicated relationship to the democratic ideal. In section 2.3, we step back from the historical narrative and pose the key question of whether, and on what terms, political equality is actually a good idea. Having identified some dangers with political equality, we conclude in section 2.4 with a look at some strategies to handle them without compromising democracy in a fundamental way.

2.1   Natural aristocracy and the mixed constitution

Histories of Western political thought often start with the writings of ancient Greek philosophers, particularly Plato (427–347 BCE) and Aristotle (384–322 BCE). Both philosophers were based in the city-state of Athens (though Aristotle was not a citizen of Athens). In Athens all political decisions were made by majority decision in a public assembly which met about forty times a year and which every adult male citizen was entitled to attend. (It is important to note that women, slaves and resident aliens or 'metics', such as Aristotle, were *not* citizens.) To enable all citizens, rich and poor, to go to the assembly, and to help ensure that each meeting was quorate, attendance was publicly subsidized from early in the fourth century BCE. The agenda for the assembly was set by a smaller body, the Council of 500, selected randomly by lot, but so as to ensure balanced representation of the ten tribes that officially made up the Athenian people. Every attendee had the right to address the assembly. Each citizen was also eligible to serve in the city's jury system. Athens had about 6,000 jurors at any one time, selected by lot from volunteers. Jury service was also subsidized. Citizens could bring cases against each other in the courts, and trials would be decided by large juries of 200–1,000 citizens (large juries are harder to bribe or intimidate). Clearly, the citizens of Athens practised a very direct form of self-government and Athens was widely seen by commentators of the day, and is still often referred to, as a 'democracy' (for a more detailed account, see Woodruff, 2005).

The democracy was, however, a highly controversial form of government. In the last third of the fifth century BCE, Athens was involved in a drawn-out war with its rival, Sparta. The war put a considerable strain on Athens, and the democracy was briefly overthrown in 414 BCE and again in 404 BCE. In the latter case, the democracy was temporarily replaced by an oligarchical regime known as 'the Thirty'. Perhaps the most infamous trial in Athens' history, the trial of Socrates on charges of blasphemy and corrupting the youth of the city, took place shortly after the restoration of the democracy. Although Socrates had not cooperated with the Thirty, the anti-democratic faction included a number of his friends and associates. In the eyes of some citizens, Socrates' philosophical teachings were seen as encouraging anti-democratic sentiments and as a threat to the stability of the restored democracy.

As a young man, Plato was a student of Socrates and, as presented in Plato's dialogues, Socrates' attitude to the democracy is one of puzzlement, bordering on scepticism.[1] In the *Protagoras* dialogue, for instance, Socrates draws a contrast between the way the democracy approaches 'technical' and 'political' decisions. In the case of technical decisions, such as how to build a bridge, experts are consulted. If a non-expert raises his voice to influence a decision he is shouted down. But, for political decisions, any citizen can get up in the assembly and have his say and expect to be listened to (Plato, 1996, 319a–e, pp. 15–16). In the context of the dialogue, Socrates takes the validity of this practice as a given. But the contrast prompts (and is perhaps intended by the author, Plato, to prompt) a question: Are political decisions in fact really different to technical ones? Should they in fact be left to the citizenry as a whole, or should they also be put in the hands of appropriate experts? As we shall see, Plato himself argues in later work that political judgment does rest on a particular kind of educable skill and that the power of political judgment should rest with those who are best endowed with the talent to develop this skill.

Some of Socrates' scepticism about democracy also comes through in the *Gorgias*. In this dialogue Socrates criticizes the practice of oratory and, by implication, raises doubts about the desirability of the democracy. Oratory is 'the ability to speak and convince the masses', the skill of speaking to a mass audience so as to produce in it a commitment to a belief that the orator wishes the mass to have (Plato, 2004, 452e–453a, 455a, pp. 12–13, 16). As such, it is a highly valuable skill to have in a democratic polity, enabling the orator to use the assembly to win the commitment of the citizenry. But oratory offers no real insight into what is right and wrong; it is the power to persuade large groups without any necessary reference to what is genuinely good (Plato, 2004, 464b–466a, pp. 32–3). To the extent that democracies leave decision-making vulnerable to the manipulations of orators, it gives power to people who cannot be relied upon to show the citizenry where its good really lies. Citizens will be misled by orators who 'pander' to them instead of leading them to do what is right. One can see Plato's *The Apology* as offering some confirmation of this thesis (Plato, 1981, pp. 23–44). This work recounts the trial of Socrates at the hands of a mass Athenian jury. Socrates is found guilty of crimes against the state and condemned to death. Is this not evidence in itself of the opposition between democracy and philosophy, between the will of the people and the claims of wisdom?

Plato shared Socrates' scepticism regarding the democracy and in his later work, particularly his *Republic*, develops an account of a radical alternative. The central organizing theme of the *Republic* is the nature of justice. Plato argues that justice at the level of the person consists in a right ordering of the three elements of the soul (Plato, 1992, 435–45, pp. 110–21). Reason should control and harness our spirit-edness or willpower so as to keep a healthy, constructive control over our appetites. Justice in the polity requires a similar ordering of social classes. At the top should stand a philosophical Guardian class. This class should have law-making power and should head a second military class of Auxiliaries who will defend and protect the state. Farmers, artisans and merchants constitute a third class who will manage the economic life of the city under the rule of the Guardians. Underlying Plato's model of the just state is a set of assumptions about social functions. Each city has various needs, such as for food, security and good government. The city works best and is just when people specialize in meeting specific needs according to their respective aptitudes and abil-ities (Plato, 1992, 374b–c, 443c, pp. 44, 119). Government is one line of specialization along with others, and the city will work best when the function of government has been put in the hands of those with greatest aptitude for this kind of work, and who have been specially trained to draw out their abilities for this task, rather than being left in the hands of the citizenry as a whole. These people will not be the orators who tend to flourish in a democracy, but those with real insight into the nature of the good – philosophers:

> Until philosophers rule as kings or those who now rule as kings and leading men genuinely and adequately philoso-phize, that is, until political philosophy and power entirely coincide . . . cities will have no rest from evils. (Plato, 1992, 473c–d, p. 148)

On this view, democracy is unjust because it involves the mass of people claiming a right to carry out a specific func-tion, government, for which they lack the right philosophical aptitude and training. Its as if everyone decided they were qualified to be a brain surgeon regardless of their knowledge or skill; or, on the analogy with the individual soul, it is as if we allowed our appetites to dictate our actions instead of reason. In a just society, then, political authority will be dis-tributed *unequally*, being held exclusively in the hands of those most qualified in terms of aptitude and training. This is the vision of the good polity as a *natural aristocracy*.

According to Plato, the rulers who make up the natural aristocracy must use myths to explain their position to the less
enlightened:

> 'All of you in the city are brothers,' we'll say to them in telling
> our story, 'but the god who made you mixed some gold into
> those who are adequately equipped to rule, because they are
> most valuable. He put silver in those who are auxiliaries and
> iron and bronze in the farmers and other craftsmen. For the
> most part you will produce children like yourselves, but,
> because you are all related, a silver child will occasionally be
> born from a golden parent, and vice versa, and all the others
> from each other. So the first and most important command
> from the god to the rulers is that there is nothing they must
> guard better or watch more carefully than the mixture of
> metals in the souls of the next generation ... for there is an
> oracle which says that the city will be ruined if it ever has an
> iron or a bronze guardian.' (Plato, 1992, 415a–c, pp. 91–2)

It is important to emphasize that Plato's Guardian class are
a ruling class but they are not an exploiting class. Their role
is to govern according to the welfare of the city as a whole
(Plato, 1992, 420b–421c, pp. 95–6). To ensure their public-
spiritedness, all Guardians receive a special education, are
monitored for bad behaviour as they grow up and in their
early adult years, and are forbidden to hold private property
or to have their own families (Plato, 1992, 377a–417b, pp.
52–93, 459a–464d, pp. 133–9). Moreover, as the passage
above indicates, Guardianship is not an inherited status. Children born from Guardian parents are excluded if they prove
unworthy, while children of lower classes can rise into the
ranks of the Guardians if they show the right aptitude.
Similarly, if they show they have the ability, women may
be Guardians as well as men (Plato, 1992, 454c–456c, pp.
128–30). In these respects, Plato's ideal state embodies in the
political sphere a form of meritocracy, a concept we will look
at in more depth in chapter 3.

Aristotle's political theory is very different in temper to
that of Plato. While Plato expends great energy developing
an elaborate picture of an ideal aristocratic society, Aristotle,
a student of Plato's, is less concerned in his *Politics* with the
ideal state than with the question of what would make for a

reasonably good state in the circumstances in which most cities find themselves. He certainly shares with Plato the idea that some people properly have authority to command others. In particular, he views the household as a site of natural authority relationships (Aristotle, 1948, book 1, chapters 3–13). Some people, with limited intellectual capacities, are 'natural slaves', and the head of each household is the proper 'master' of a group of these natural slaves. The male head of household also has proper authority over his children and, in addition, over his wife. The polity is an association of male householders; those subordinate to male householders, such as natural slaves, children and wives, do not have the status of citizens and so do not have membership of the polity except via their male head. But what about the political relationship amongst these male heads of household? Does democracy apply here in Aristotle's view? Or does Aristotle support a natural aristocracy like Plato's?

One of the central ideas of Aristotle's *Ethics* is that of the 'golden mean', and in this political context too Aristotle for the most part treads a middle path between Plato and the Athenian democrat. In principle, Aristotle agrees that the state ought to be a genuine aristocracy, that those who are in government should be those with a natural aptitude for virtuous living and who receive the training to make the most of their potential (Aristotle, 1948, book 4, chapter 7, books 7–8). But most cities are not founded in conditions which make this feasible. In the vast majority of real-world cities, the lawmaker must aim for something less ambitious. He should aim for a political system that combines elements of oligarchy and aristocracy on the one hand with elements of democracy on the other (Aristotle, 1948, book 4, chapters 8–9, 11–13).

To see the sort of thing that Aristotle has in mind here, imagine a city that we will call New Athens. In New Athens every free citizen (let us say, every non-metic male householder) has a right to vote for people to represent him in the city's lawmaking assembly. However, only those with wealth above a certain high threshold are eligible to stand for election to this assembly. New Athens is not a democracy because lawmaking power is confined to the rich; in this respect, it has a strong oligarchic element. But it is not straightforwardly an oligarchy either. For, while lawmaking power lies in the hands of the rich, individual rich men need the votes of the less affluent to get elected to the lawmaking assembly. In such a situation, neither rich nor poor are likely to have unqualified control of the city. The poor cannot dominate because they never get their hands directly on the levers of power. The rich cannot dominate because, as individuals, they may not get elected to the body with lawmaking power unless they can appeal to a section of the poorer classes, and this will pressure them to take their interests into account.[2] Plato's basic idea is that we should promote good government, that serves the welfare of the city as a whole, by reserving political authority to the wise and virtuous (a natural aristocracy). Aristotle's basic idea is that in the circumstances of most cities we should promote good government, that serves the welfare of the city as a whole, by carefully dividing political authority between rich and poor (and other social groups).[3]

In place of the idea of natural aristocracy we have the idea of a *mixed constitution*: mixed in terms of how it combines aspects of oligarchy and aristocracy on the one hand and democracy on the other. Political authority is, again, distributed unequally; in the imaginary case of New Athens the average rich citizen has a greater share of authority than the average poor citizen. But the inequality is not as severe as in Plato's ideal state where political authority is the exclusive property of the Guardian class.

Aristotle's idea of the mixed constitution has exercised considerable long-term influence in political thought. A particularly important development of the idea was provided by the Greek historian Polybius, writing about 150 years after Aristotle (Polybius, 1979). Polybius argued that there is a natural cycle in the development of political regimes. Starting out as monarchies (individual rulers serving the good of the city as a whole), regimes degenerate in time into tyrannies (individual rulers serving their own interests at the city's expense); this provokes a revolt by other major figures in society, leading to the establishment of aristocracies (an elite group ruling in the city's interests) which, in time, degenerate into oligarchies (an elite group ruling in its own interests at the expense of the city); this provokes a popular revolt which establishes a democracy; but this quickly becomes unstable and prompts a return to 'strong man' leadership, a new monarchy. And thus the cycle starts again. However, in some cases the cycle might work in a slightly different way. Instead of displacing monarchy, a form of aristocracy emerges as a counterweight to monarchy/tyranny; and, in time, an element of democracy is added to the regime as a counterweight to aristocracy/oligarchy. The result is a truly mixed constitution combining elements of monarchy, aristocracy and democracy, each component serving to limit the potential flaws of the others. Polybius explained the success of republican Rome in terms of its approximation to this model of the mixed constitution. Much later, humanist thinkers of the early modern period, such as Niccolò Machiavelli and James Harrington, took up this view and, in their distinctive ways, advocated a brand of government based on variations on the idea of the mixed constitution derived from Aristotle and Polybius (Machiavelli, 1970 [1531], especially book 1, chapter 2; Harrington, 1992 [1656]). In Machiavelli's words:

> prudent legislators, aware of their defects, refrained from adopting as such any one of these forms [monarchy, aristocracy, democracy], and chose instead one that shared in them all, since they thought such a government would be stronger and more stable, for if in one and the same state there was principality, aristocracy and democracy each would keep watch over the other. (Machiavelli, 1970 [1531], p. 109)

2.2 The social contract and political equality

In reading Plato and Aristotle one is struck by how far they affirm the principle of natural authority: that some people naturally have authority over others in view of their higher capacities (particularly their higher capacity for reason). By no means all of their contemporaries agreed with them: in the dialogue *Protagoras*, the philosopher of this name argues that all men are endowed by the gods with an educable capacity for intelligent moral judgment which is why they can reasonably claim a more or less equal share in the exercise of political authority. In the context of the constitutional crisis of the English Civil Wars, some radicals on the Parliamentarian side emerged to issue a new challenge to conventional views about the naturalness of authority relationships. In the words of the Leveller, John Lilburne, writing in 1646, all men are 'by nature equal and alike in power, dignity, authority, and majesty – none of them having (by nature) any authority, dominion or magisterial power, one over or above another' (Lilburne, in Sharp (ed.), 1998, p. 31). No person – or at least no 'man' – is born subject to the authority of another. Each man has a proper sovereignty over his own self. In the words of John Milton: 'No man who knows aught, can be so stupid to deny that all men naturally were born free, being the image and resemblance of God himself, and were by privilege above all the creatures, born to command and not to obey' (Milton, in Wallace (ed.), 1925 [1649], p. 331). But the word 'man' here is significant: most of the thinkers we will discuss in this section agree with Aristotle on the natural authority of men over women and, on this basis, mostly accepted the exclusion of women from political citizenship (Okin, 1979, chapters 5–8; Pateman, 1988).

The idea of natural equality (that is, the absence of natural authority) went hand in hand with growing interest in the *social contract theory* of political legitimacy. This says that a system of political authority has moral legitimacy if it is, or if under ideal circumstances it plausibly could be, the outcome of a joint contract to establish a shared system of political authority by those who are bound to obey the commands of this authority.[4] Those employing this approach, in its hypothetical form, ask: If people were in an appropriate initial situation – for instance, one which expresses their moral equality – would they agree to form a state and, if so, what kind of state would they agree to form? The answer given to this question then allegedly provides a benchmark against which to judge the legitimacy of the state we in fact have. As Jean Hampton puts it: 'the social contract theorist figuratively takes the state apart and (rationally) puts it back together again in order to explain the structure of any existing state and to determine whether or not it is justified' (Hampton, 1986, p. 269). Social contract theories were a salient feature of political argument in the

English seventeenth century, with notable contributions not only from the Levellers but from Thomas Hobbes and John Locke.

In approaching the social contract tradition, it is very important to make a distinction between the idea of what we might term contractual equality and the idea of political equality. By contractual equality, we mean the equal standing of the various parties who come together in the contract situation (actual or hypothetical) to establish a political system. Political equality refers to the status of people within the political system that is established by the contract. It obtains when each member of a political system has more or less an equal share in the power to issue binding commands on the citizenry as a whole. All the social contract theories we shall consider express the idea of contractual equality. But this does not mean that the theorists all endorse the idea of political equality. Some argue that the people should or may contract for something else.

Hobbes and Locke provide two good examples. In his book, *Leviathan* (1985 [1651]), Hobbes argues that, in order to escape a chaotic world in which life is continually under threat, we would agree to establish a political authority to lay down the law and punish people who transgress it. But, according to Hobbes, the kind of political system we would find it most rational to set up is an absolute monarchy: a system where one person has unqualified authority to rule over everyone else. Hobbes suggests that anything less will jeopardize the stability we seek when we establish a political system.[5] The contract he proposes is essentially a contract of mutual subjugation, in which people agree to follow the commands of a single person, the absolute monarch, so as to escape the violence of a world without settled authority (Hampton, 1986, chapters 4–7). It is important to see that Hobbes completely rejects Plato's idea that some people have a natural authority over others based on superior wisdom. Like Lilburne, Milton, and other radicals in the Civil War period, Hobbes believes that we are all naturally independent of any other person's authority. But this does not lead Hobbes to endorse political equality. None of us is born the subject of others, morally speaking; but we should use the natural freedom we have to subject ourselves to a shared monarch as quickly as we can. For it is better to live under someone as master than to die in our freedom.

Locke's political theory, as set out in his *Two Treatises of Government* (1960 [1689]), is in part a reply to Hobbes. Like Lilburne and Milton, Locke agrees that men have natural freedom, that no man is simply born the subject of another. A legitimate system of government is therefore founded on the consent of those who are subject to it. Locke's model of the social contract can helpfully be broken down into three stages. In stage one, a group of people make the decision to form a political association: that is, an association under which they will be subject to a shared authority. No person can be considered a member of the association without their individual consent. In stage two, the people who have agreed to form a political association decide what type of government they should establish. At this point, decisions are to follow the principle of majority rule. In Locke's words:

> For when any number of Men have, by the consent of every individual, made a *Community*, they have thereby made that *Community* one Body, with a Power to act as one Body, which is only the will and determination of the *majority*. For that which acts any Community, being only the consent of the individuals of it, and it being necessary to that which is one body to move one way; it is necessary the Body should move that way whither the greater force carries it, which is the *consent of the majority*. (Locke, Laslett (ed.), 1960 [1689], p. 375).

In stage three, finally, the people who have made the social contract set about living under the political system agreed to at stage two. But what kind of political system is this? Locke is clear that it cannot be the kind of absolute monarchy that Hobbes advocates. Such a system leaves the subject far too vulnerable to the whims of a single person. But, beyond this, Locke leaves it fairly open as to what kind of regime is established at stage two. What he certainly does not argue is that the regime established for stage three should itself embody the democratic character that decision-making has in stage two of the social contract. While the people at stage two have equal votes in deciding what political system to establish, with disagreement being resolved by majority rule, Locke does not argue that they ought to choose a political system that itself embodies this equality and operates on the basis of majority rule.[6] Thus, once again, the idea of contractual equality does not carry over into a defence of political equality.

However, other contractualist theorists did advocate political equality, or at least something close to it (and even then for men, and not women). One group who took a large step in this direction were the aforementioned Levellers. Based in London and in the New Model Army that defeated the king, Charles I, in the English Civil War, the Levellers pressed for a wholly new constitution in settlement of this conflict. To emphasize the idea that a legitimate political system is founded on the consent of those subject to its authority they termed their proposals, *An Agreement of the People* (1647, in Sharp (ed.), 1998, pp. 92–101). The Levellers called for authority to lie with Parliament (rather than the king) and for biannual elections to the Parliament in which all – or at least most – adult males would have an equal vote.[7] Like Locke and Hobbes, then, the Levellers believed legitimate authority should rest on a social contract in which each person is an equal associate. But, unlike Hobbes and Locke, they were sure that the political system established through the contract – the 'agreement of the people' – should itself embody the equality of the contract situation. Contractual equality and political equality go together. The Levellers preceded Hobbes and Locke – the *Agreement* dates from 1647, Hobbes's *Leviathan* from 1651, and Locke's *Two Treatises* from the 1680s – and it is possible to see Hobbes and Locke as two thinkers who, in different ways, were seeking to preserve the social contract theory of political legitimacy while detaching it from the Leveller commitment to political equality.

An Agreement of the People was debated at a meeting of the New Model Army's General Council in October 1647 (the Putney Debates). Here the *Agreement* provoked strong opposition from leading figures of the army, such as Oliver Cromwell and Henry Ireton, who saw in the arguments and proposals of the Levellers a philosophical challenge and practical danger to private property. In Ireton's view, the right to share in authority ought to be conditional on property ownership:

> I think that no person has a right to an interest or share in
> the disposing or determining of the affairs of the kingdom,
> and in choosing those that shall determine what laws we shall
> be ruled by here . . . that has not a permanent fixed interest in
> this kingdom [that is, property in land] . . . that by a man's
> being born here he shall have a share in that power that shall
> dispose of the lands here, and of all the things here, I do not
> think it a sufficient ground. (Sharp (ed.), 1998, pp. 103–4)

The corollary of this is that the poor are excluded from
political rights and have to trust the propertied classes to rule
in a way that respects their interests as well as those of the
better off. This means, however, that the poor man lives
according to the will of the richer man. He is, in this sense,
akin to a slave rather than being a free person (Skinner,
1998). And yet: the poor man may have just as much capacity for making laws as the rich man. The poor man has a
capacity for intelligent judgment and for commitment to the
public good – he has what Thomas Rainborough, an eloquent
supporter of the Levellers in the Putney Debates, calls '[t]his
gift of reason without other property' (Sharp (ed.), 1998, p.
106). One of the Levellers' key ideas was that by denying the
poor man equality in political rights one thereby failed properly to acknowledge his status as a reasonable being, as much
made in the image of God as the rich man. It was perhaps
partly in this spirit that Rainborough incredulously summed
up Ireton's argument thus: 'I am a poor man, therefore I must
be *oppressed*?' (Sharp, 1998, p. 109; see also the passage at
the head of this chapter).[8]
    While Hobbes and Locke detached the social contract
idea from the democratic ideas of the Levellers, one later
social contract theorist, Jean-Jacques Rousseau, forcefully
reasserted the link. In his *The Social Contract* (1994 [1762]),
Rousseau begins with a firm repudiation of the Aristotelian
idea of natural authority:

> Aristotle too had said . . . that men are not naturally equal,
> but that some are born for slavery and some for mastery.
>   Aristotle was right, but he took the effect for the
> cause. Any man who is born in slavery is born for
> slavery. . . . Slaves in their chains lose everything, even the
> desire to be rid of them. . . . If there are slaves by nature, it is

because slaves have been made against nature. (book 1, chapter 2, p. 47)

If men are treated like slaves, they will develop a character suited to this status. But no man is a slave in his genes, as it were; each person has the potential to be a free and responsible being. Enslavement is a violation of this potential. Political association should not be conceived as an arrangement between a group of masters and a group of slaves, then, but as a consensual association of free men. Moreover, in forming the political association, each man will properly wish to preserve his freedom. He will wish to remain 'as free as before' and 'obey himself alone' (book 1, chapter 6). But how can this be done? How can people be subject to shared laws and yet remain obedient to their own wills? According to Rousseau, this is possible only if the citizens who have to obey the laws also themselves make the laws (see J. Cohen, forthcoming, for elaboration of this idea). Thus, he argues, the social contract must be understood as an agreement amongst the contracting parties to put themselves under the authority of an assembly of the whole people. The contract is an agreement to set up a political system in which all lawmaking power lies with this citizen assembly, and to follow the laws which are made in this citizen assembly.

It may help to contrast Rousseau's social contract with Locke's. Recall that for Locke, in what I termed stage two of the contract, all the contracting parties are involved in agreeing the kind of political system they are to live under in stage three. The decision is based on majority rule with each contractor having an equal vote. But, in Locke's view, the political system that applies in stage three need not mirror the simple equality of stage two. In essence, Rousseau is suggesting that the political system applicable in stage three must be a continuation of the system at work in stage two. In a real sense, for Rousseau, *we must never leave stage two*. We must remain, permanently, in a political system in which the basic terms of civil association are under the review of an assembly of the whole citizenry. Of course, Rousseau does not mean that we should literally sit in such an assembly the whole time. We have work to do and lives to lead. But he does think that laws may only be made through such an assembly, and that the assembly must meet relatively frequently to review the laws. Above all, the citizens may not delegate the making of their laws to a group of representatives (Rousseau, 1994 [1762], book 3, chapter 15). For this would compromise the freedom of the citizen: in obeying the laws, he would now be subject not to his own will, as declared in an assembly of the whole citizenry, but to the will of another (the representative). In this respect, Rousseau's position is distinct from, and even more egalitarian than, that of the Levellers who argued for political equality (or something close to it) expressed through the election of a representative assembly.

Another feature of Rousseau's model of democracy should be noted. Even if all the citizens who stand to be bound by society's laws take part in making them, it does not necessarily follow from this alone, of course, that each citizen ends up willing the laws he is required to obey. Some self-interested group in the assembly might win a majority for a law that damages my basic interests (for example, it might adopt an economic system that I foresee will lead to me suffering acute poverty). I cannot be expected to vote for such a law. This point leads Rousseau to emphasize – as, in fact, the Levellers did before him – that democratic citizens must enter into the lawmaking process in a public-spirited fashion. Specifically, for Rousseau, in making laws citizens must not seek their own good in a way that comes at the expense of the basic interests of others, but in a way that gives equal weight to the basic interests of others (see J. Cohen, forthcoming). (If I demand a right to private property, for instance, then it must be on terms that are compatible with all other citizens having adequate access to private property.) If citizens approach lawmaking in this spirit, then there is more likelihood that the laws will be able to command the genuine support of the citizenry as a whole, as it is likely nobody will have cause to feel unfairly done down.[9]

We might call this the *moralized conception of democracy*. On this conception, democracy is not simply a matter of every citizen having an equal say in making laws. It is a matter of citizens having an equal say in a process that is consciously aimed at finding laws that serve the interests of the citizenry as a whole, that are fair to all citizens – where our sense of fairness is informed by the principle of moral equality. The citizen of a moralized democracy will have to ask of a given proposed law or electoral candidate: 'Can I vote for this law or candidate given that I have a responsibility to seek laws that treat others fairly?'. In the view of Rousseau and other moralized democrats, the rights associated with political equality come with a moral responsibility to use these rights in this morally constrained way (see Rousseau, 1994 [1762], book 4, chapter 1, p. 135).

Again, here we come back to the idea of the social contract. For one way the citizen of a moralized democracy might explore the issue of whether proposed laws and policies are fair to all, considered as moral equals, is for her to ask whether she thinks that the laws and policies, or the principles used to justify them, are such that they could be the focus of a social contract. Could every citizen agree to them, given a shared willingness to find laws that are agreeable to all? The social contract, writes the philosopher Immanuel Kant:

> is an *idea* of reason, which nonetheless has undoubted practical reality; for it can oblige every legislator to frame his laws in such a way that they could have been produced by the united will of a whole nation. . . . This is the test of rightfulness of every public law. (Kant, 1991 [1793], p. 79)

In contemporary philosophy, the most influential version of this idea is presented in John Rawls's *A Theory of Justice*, first published in 1971, and recently revised (Rawls, 1999a). Rawls asks us to imagine a contract situation in which people have to choose principles for the design of their society behind what he calls a 'veil of ignorance' which deprives them of knowledge of their own likely position in society. Citizens of a democracy can perhaps get a sense of what principles are fair to all by asking themselves honestly what principles they think people would choose in this original position (J. Cohen, 2003). The veil of ignorance serves as a way of getting us to consider how the social world looks from all positions in society, not just the sort of position we expect to occupy, and hence helps us look at things in a way that is more impartial, and more consistent with respecting the moral equality of citizens (we will discuss Rawls's theory in more detail in chapter 5). Other contemporary philosophers have proposed alternative versions of this kind of social contract thought-experiment (Barry, 1995; see also Nagel, 1979, 1991; Scanlon, 1999). Thus there is a sense in which the moralized democrat agrees with Plato when he says that 'philosophy and power should coincide': as a *moralized* democrat, she is keen for the citizen to be engaged with the philosophical question of what is fair to all, possibly employing social contract thought-experiments to help work out and defend her views; as a moralized *democrat*, however, she insists that the question be one that engages the whole community, not simply an elite Guardian class.

2.3   Why democracy?

In this section I want to step back a little from the historical trajectory sketched in sections 2.1 and 2.2 and think about the underlying considerations that support the case for political equality. Is political equality justified? If so, on what grounds? And subject to what (if any) qualifications?

The political process has both an 'input' and an 'output' side. On the input side we stand as citizens more or less involved in the process of making laws and policies. On the output side we stand as subjects who are bound by laws and as people whose interests are profoundly affected by them. As Charles Beitz has argued, in considering the justification of political equality we need to consider the issue both from the input and output sides, from the standpoint of the citizen as a potential maker of laws and from that of the subject as the recipient of them (Beitz, 1989).

Now if we start by looking at the issue from the input side, political equality might be defended in terms of what I shall call the *respect argument*. A premise of the argument is that, as Protagoras insisted to Socrates, all people have a capacity (at least, a latent capacity) for intelligent moral judgment. The twentieth-century philosopher John Rawls similarly speaks of the idea that citizens share certain 'moral powers', including a 'capacity for a sense of justice' (Rawls, 1993,

p. 19).[10] Or, as the Levellers might have put it, reaching for the religious language of their time, each man is made in the image of God and, as such, has an innate capacity for making judgments about right and wrong in both private and public contexts. This makes men equals in a fundamental way. By excluding some from political rights we fail to recognize this fundamental equality, based on shared moral capacity, and so show disrespect towards the men (people) who are excluded. The force of the respect argument is seen plainly if, for example, we consider the demand for political equality as an alternative to basing political rights on property. In a society where the right to vote and hold political office is confined to members of the propertied classes, a person in the lower social classes might say to themselves: 'I am just as good a judge of the common good as that rich person. So why should I have no vote or right to hold office while he does?' Of course, if people are denied the opportunity to exercise their capacity for intelligent moral judgment on public affairs, as they are in undemocratic polities, then, in the case of many people, this capacity will probably be underdeveloped. But if our political institutions do give people this opportunity, then, so the argument goes, their latent capacities will come through. Those, like Plato, who say that most people simply do not have such capacities allegedly make the same mistake that Rousseau identifies in Aristotle's theory of natural slavery: they confuse the effects of unjust social institutions with the effects of nature.

Not only does the denial of political equality arguably express disrespect in itself, but by doing so it could also impact more generally on the social status of individuals. Those excluded from equal political rights might well be seen by others, and may well feel themselves, to be inferior in a fundamental and comprehensive sense. Thus, the denial of political equality might also undermine status equality and, with it, the self-respect of those relegated to the inferior social status (see Beitz, 1989, pp. 109–10).

Let's now turn to the output side of government. On this side, political equality can also be defended in terms of what we may call the *consequence argument*. According to this argument, political equality is uniquely desirable because a political system based on political equality tends to produce outputs of law and policy that have better consequences for society than other systems: a system based on political equality will tend to generate laws and policies that better serve social welfare and/or make society more just. Utilitarian theorists of the early nineteenth century, such as Jeremy Bentham and James Mill, based their case for universal manhood suffrage on a specific version of this argument, claiming that it would be more likely to produce policies that maximize total happiness (Mill, 1978 [1824/5]). Note that we need not choose between the respect and consequence arguments. We might ground our case for political equality in an appeal to a range of arguments (Cohen and Sabel, 1997).

Let's now consider the merits of these arguments, starting with the consequence argument. There certainly are some reasons for thinking that representative democracies tend to have beneficial consequences compared to non-democratic systems. For example, severe economic crises, such as famines, are less likely in democratic countries than in non-democratic ones: 'no substantial famine has ever occurred in any independent country with a democratic form of government and a relatively free press' (Sen, 1999, p. 152; see also pp. 180–4). Democratic countries are also less likely to go to war with one another than non-democratic countries are (Dahl, 1998, pp. 57–8). Both effects can probably be explained in part by the greater *accountability* of decision-making to ordinary people in a representative democracy. In non-democratic systems, decision-makers are not under the same degree of pressure to accommodate ordinary people's wants as in a democratic system and this makes them more able to pursue policies that inflict great costs on ordinary citizens, such as those involved in famine and war.

Further support for the consequence argument is provided at the theoretical level by the eighteenth-century French political thinker, the Marquis de Condorcet. Condorcet asks us to imagine a group of people – a 'jury' – whose task is to deliver a judgment on an issue where there is a right and wrong answer (such as whether a person is guilty of a crime). If we assume that each member of the jury has a higher than 50 per cent probability of getting the right answer (or even just that, with an evenly balanced or 'normal' distribution, the average probability is above 50 per cent), then it can be shown that as the number of people on the jury increases, the probability of a majority vote giving the objectively right answer also increases; indeed, it approaches 100 per cent quite quickly. This result, known as Condorcet's Jury Theorem, is very important (Grofman and Feld, 2002 [1988]; see also Przeworski, 1999). It shows that even if most citizens are fallible in their judgments about what laws or policies it is right to adopt (or what candidates it is right to elect), provided they tend to be more right than wrong on average, then under certain conditions, we will have good reason to think that their collective decision, taken on the basis of voting equality, is the right one. If they are making judgments with reference to the common good, say, then their collective judgment can be relied upon to track what does indeed promote the common good, with beneficial consequences for society.

However, returning to Condorcet's result, one key assumption is that the jurors have, at the very least on average, a higher than 50 per cent chance of voting the right way. But if the average probability is less than 50 per cent, which is at least conceivable, then the logic works in reverse and we would do well to limit the number of people involved in decision-making.

In addition, our first point about democratic accountability cuts two ways. Many policies that inflict great costs on the citizenry are indeed bad policies, and so if democratic accountability helps to prevent such policies, then democracy has good consequences. However, some policies that imply a significant sacrifice for citizens may actually be the right policies to adopt (not because the sacrifice itself is good, but because it is the price of achieving something that is more valuable). If democratic accountability blocks such a policy, then democracy helps produce bad consequences. A contemporary example might be environmental policy. It can be argued that the only way to get to grips with the world's growing environmental problems, in a globally fair way, requires the citizens of richer nations to accept cuts in their living standards (Barry, 2005, chapters 19–20). But no democratic politician feels able to stand for election on such a platform as they would be routed at the polls. In this case, democracy might work against the long-term welfare of society (or against justice to people in other nations). It is at least possible that a less democratic system of government could make quicker progress in adopting the painful, but right, policies.

In fact, many political thinkers who have broadly supported the arrival of democracy in the modern world have nevertheless worried about its potentially bad consequences. Two 'anxious democrats' of this kind are Alexis de Tocqueville and John Stuart Mill. In his two-volumed *Democracy in America*, Tocqueville analysed the dangers inherent in a 'democratic' society characterized by social and political equality. The principle of majority rule could too easily turn into what he calls the 'tyranny of the majority':

> When I see that the right and the means of absolute command are conferred on any power whatever, be it called a people or a king, an aristocracy or a democracy, a monarchy or a republic, I say there is the germ of tyranny, and I seek to live elsewhere. (Tocqueville, 1990 [1835], p. 260)

Mill reviewed Tocqueville's volumes and shared his concerns. In his *On Representative Government*, Mill defends the principle of popular participation in lawmaking and government on the grounds that it fosters the development of an active, creative, problem-solving type of character: 'there can be no doubt that the passive type of character is favoured by the government of the one or a few, and the active self-helping type by that of the Many' (Mill, 1993b [1861], p. 231). But his *On Liberty* expresses a profound concern that majorities might use their power in a democracy to stifle the 'experiments in living' favoured by a minority of citizens with a more creative character (Mill, 1985 [1859]).

The consequence argument for political equality is, then, a strong argument but not a conclusive one. Does the respect argument fare any better?

One obvious challenge to the respect argument follows directly from the point that a political system based on political equality can have very bad, as well as good, consequences. Imagine you know that an ethnic majority will use its equal voting rights to make laws that persecute the members of an ethnic minority. However, you are in a position to put a political system in place which gives you, or some other Guardian, the power to veto laws of this kind. If you do, you can help to prevent gross violation of basic human rights, but you also override political equality. Should you put this system of Guardianship in place? Appealing to the notion of 'respect' does not give an unambiguous answer. This is because the demand for respect arises not only in connection with our power to make an input into the making of laws and policy, but in connection with the outputs of the political process. If the outputs are morally very bad, then they will typically fail to show some people the respect they are due. So, in the kind of case I have described, we apparently have a claim to respect on the input side of the political system conflicting with a claim to respect on the output side. It is by no means clear that the respect claim on the input side should always trump that on the output side; that is, it is by no means clear that democratic political rights should always be upheld at the expense of other rights if there is a conflict. As Beitz suggests, one can think of the issue in terms of the idea of the social contract: if we are contracting with others to establish a political system we will properly want to consider how alternatives could affect people's interests on both the input and output side (Beitz, 1989, pp. 97–117).

Are there ways in which we might structure a system based on political equality so as to minimize the dangers of majority rule? Are there ways in which we can have a fundamental political equality on the input side while also protecting individuals from gross injustice on the output side? If so, then systems of this specific kind might well be the kind that social contractors can reasonably sign up to.

2.4 Majority tyranny: two protective strategies

In his *Democracy in America*, Tocqueville identifies a number of ways in which nineteenth-century American democracy reduces the risk of majority tyranny. He is struck by the role played by courts in evaluating legislation, and with the wider influence of the legal profession, which represents in his eyes a kind of 'aristocracy' within American democracy tempering popular judgment (Tocqueville, 1990 [1835], volume 1, chapter 16). He is struck also by the way American citizens are active in managing public affairs at the local level. Participation in juries and in local government pulls people out of the private sphere and helps to develop the skills and sensibilities of responsible democratic citizenship (Tocqueville, 1990 [1835], volume 1, chapter 16, [1840], volume 2, book 2, chapter 4). These two specific observations correspond to two protective strategies against majority tyranny which we may call the *aristocratic strategy* and the *participatory strategy*.[11] A convincing argument for either strategy would require more discussion than I provide here, and they are not the only strategies one can conceive, but both look to have some promise. At base, both strategies aim to improve outputs from democratic decision-making by encouraging more informed and public-spirited deliberation on policy issues.

1. *The aristocratic strategy.* To prevent majority tyranny many people argue that we should plump for a 'constitutional' or 'liberal' democracy in which the power of majority rule is constrained by a constitutional Bill of Rights or Basic Law, backed up by the institution of judicial review. In the United States, for example, laws are made by Congress and the state legislatures which are elected in competitive elections based on universal suffrage. However, citizens can appeal to the courts to establish that a given law, passed by Congress or a state legislature, is inconsistent with the individual rights enumerated in the federal constitution. If their appeal is upheld, then the law is invalidated. So do we here have a system in which lawmaking is in the hands of the people, yet the individual has some protection against majority tyranny?

In fact, it is not clear that we do. Even if the constitution is authorized by the people as a whole (and when *was* the United States Constitution last authorized by the people?), the meaning of constitution texts is far from clear. This raises the issue of who is to give the authoritative interpretation of the constitution. In the United States, this authority rests with the Supreme Court, an unelected body of nine men and women. So it might be argued that ultimate authority to say what counts as a valid law in the United States rests not with the people, who are supposedly sovereign, but with these nine men and women. Of course, these nine men and women are ideally people of learning and expertise (one stresses the word 'ideally'). But, so the critics might say, to cede authority to the 'wise' in this way is to shift away from democracy in the direction of a form of Guardianship (Dahl, 1958, 1998; Kramer, 2004; Tushnet, 2005). The system is not fundamentally democratic but represents a mixed constitution of the kind proposed by Aristotle: the people has the power to initiate laws, but an aristocracy based in the judiciary, particularly the Supreme Court, has the power to throw laws out if it judges them unconstitutional. According to some critics, the constitution is so open to different interpretations, the aristocracy can, in effect, throw out any law it doesn't like, rationalizing its decision by reference to the constitution. Individual rights might (or might not) be better protected, but political equality has been compromised in a fundamental way.[12]

Let us not give up too quickly, however. We need to distinguish between a court having the *power to issue a judgment* as to the compatibility of a law with the constitution, and the further *power to invalidate a law* through such a judgment. The first power need not come with the second: a negative judgment could trigger consequences that fall short of immediate, authoritative invalidation. For example, perhaps it might have the consequence that the legislature must vote on the law again within, say, a year, and that on this second occasion the proposal must win a supermajority (say, over 60 per cent of the legislature). The basic idea is that a negative judgment would require legislatures to revisit and seriously reconsider laws without striking them down once and for all (Cohen and Sabel, 1997, p. 335, Waldron, 2005). In this way politicians, and the citizenry at large, are given more time, and perhaps some important fresh reasons, to consider whether the law in question is what they want (Rawls, 2001, pp. 145–7; for a sceptical view, see Waldron, 2002).[13] It puts legislators under pressure to look closely at what they are doing and to address serious moral objections. Democratic lawmaking is supplemented here by an element of aristocracy, in the form of the courts, but it is not fundamentally compromised by it (Kramer, 2004, pp. 249–53).

2. *The participatory strategy.* A second proposed strategy for containing the dangers of democracy is participation. The basic idea is: if you want responsible citizens, then you had better give citizens some responsibility – not merely responsibility in their own individual lives, but responsibility for the management of shared, public affairs that has to be exercised in cooperation with other citizens. Participation in spheres of democratic decision-making will, it is hoped, have the effect of educating people in the skills and norms of democratic citizenship. In Mill's words, the citizen who participates in collective decision-making:

> is called upon, while so engaged, to weigh interests not his own; to be guided, in case of conflicting claims, by another rule than his private partiality; to apply, at every turn, principles and maxims which have for their reason of existence the common good: and he usually finds associated with him in the same work minds more familiarized than his own with these ideas and operations, whose study it will be to supply reasons to his understanding and stimulation to his feeling for the general interest. (Mill, 1993b [1861], p. 233–4)

In addition to Mill, versions of this thesis can be found in the works of Rousseau and Tocqueville; in those of early twentieth-century critics of mass representative democracy such as G. D. H. Cole and Mary Parker Follet (Cole, 1920; Follet, 1998 [1918]); and in the writings of contemporary democratic thinkers (Pateman, 1970, chapter 2; Fung and Wright, 2003, p. 28).[14]

Following in the spirit of Rousseau's *The Social Contract*, some have argued for participatory, direct democracy as an alternative to representative democracy. Typically, they envisage lawmaking power being devolved down to local citizen and/or workplace assemblies. In the most idealistic models, these assemblies are sovereign and independent, but may choose to federate together to handle shared problems. Representatives would be sent to meetings of higher federal bodies. But they would function under instruction from below, or would at least be instantly recallable by the lower bodies. Models of participatory democracy along these lines informed Marxist and anarchist thinking about the structure of a possible post-capitalist society (Kropotkin, 1970 [1913];

Pannekoek, 2002 [1948]). Interest in them revived with the emergence of the New Left in the 1960s, and this interest continues in some currents of the ecological movement today. Murray Bookchin, for example, argues that urgent environmental problems call for a radical reorganization of society into substantially independent municipalities which use direct democracy to manage their economic affairs (Bookchin, 1971, 1980, 2003).

However, most supporters of participatory democracy think it more desirable, or at least feasible, to build participatory democratic spheres within a political system that retains conventional national representative institutions (perhaps supplemented, for reasons set out in chapter 7, with new transnational representative institutions). Tocqueville and Mill emphasized local government and the jury system as arenas for participation (Tocqueville, 1990 [1835; 1840], volume 2, book 2, chapter 4; Mill, 1993b [1861], chapter 3). Carole Pateman and Robert Dahl have emphasized the workplace as a site of participation in decision-making (Pateman, 1970; Dahl, 1985). More recently, attention has focused on the potential for creating new spheres of participatory democratic governance to help handle specific social problems, such as control of crime, improving educational standards and workforce skills, and managing environmental problems (Cohen and Sabel, 1997; Fung and Wright, 2003; Fung, 2004).[15] Other writers have focused on the possible role that citizens' juries and deliberative opinion polls might play in bringing citizens into the discussion of policy issues in an advisory capacity to national or local government (Fishkin, 1995; Smith and Wales, 2000).[16] These writers point to a range of potential benefits from these participatory initiatives, but they all follow Mill in arguing that participation is desirable in part because of the way it allegedly develops citizens' capacities for responsible decision-making.

Thus, the aristocratic and participatory strategies both aim to reduce the risk of majority tyranny by assisting citizens in the development and exercise of their capacities for informed moral judgment on public issues. Both envisage this happening in the context of energetic, face-to-face discussion between citizens in which ideas about fairness and the public good are exchanged and examined. In this respect, both the aristocratic and participatory strategies fit into a specific model of moralized democracy which is often referred to as *deliberative democracy* (J. Cohen, 1997a, Gutmann and Thompson, 1996, 2004; Miller, 2000b).[17] In a sense, any moralized democracy is a deliberative democracy in that individual moral judgment on public issues demands some kind of inner, personal deliberation (Goodin, 2003). But deliberative democrats emphasize the importance of shared, public discussion to assist individual moral judgment.

In this contemporary ideal of deliberative democracy we see clear echoes of earlier political ideals. Insofar as the mechanisms used to nurture deliberation are participatory, deliberative democracy carries a clear echo of the direct democracy of the Athenian city-state. Insofar as the mechanisms are aristocratic, there is perhaps also a distant, fainter echo of the classical ideal of the mixed constitution.

3
Meritocracy

rank and dignity in society must take a new ground. . . .
It must now take the substantial ground of character,
instead of the chimerical ground of titles.
Tom Paine, *The Rights of Man: Part One*, 1791

In a moralized democracy, citizens seek to arrange their laws
and institutions in a way that takes the interests of all citizens
fairly into account. As part of this, they must consider
how much or what kind of social and economic inequality is
consistent with fair treatment of their fellow citizens. So far
as economic inequality is concerned, very few thinkers have
argued that fairness demands complete equality of incomes
or wealth (an exception is Shaw, 1937, pp. 54–5, 99–101).
Fairness seems more complicated than this. But if we reject
this simple principle, what is the most plausible alternative?

The quote above from Tom Paine's *The Rights of Man*
points towards one possibility. Inequality is fair, on this view,
not when it is grounded in inherited status, as it is in a traditional
aristocratic society, but when it is based on people's
real abilities and achievements (what Paine calls 'character').
This states, in a very general way, the ideal of *meritocracy*.
Applied to the economy, the ideal of meritocracy is conventionally
understood to mean that the distribution of economic
goods, such as jobs and incomes, should be governed by

economic merit as reflected in the relative productive talents and efforts of individuals. However, if people are not on a sufficiently level playing field in terms of their opportunities to compete for jobs and incomes, then the jobs and incomes may go to the less able and the less hard-working. Thus, for individual merit to shine through and earn its due reward, there must be, in some appropriate sense, *equality of opportunity*. The aim of this chapter is to take a closer look at these related notions of meritocracy and equality of opportunity.

Section 3.1 clarifies the values that are thought to support meritocracy. Sections 3.2 and 3.3 explore an important distinction between two different conceptions of meritocracy and of equality of opportunity ('weak' and 'strong' meritocracy). Section 3.4 looks at how social scientists explore the extent of meritocracy in contemporary societies and describes some of their findings. Sections 3.5–3.8 then review a range of important criticisms of the ideal of meritocracy (in both weak and strong forms): that achieving the ideal would require too great a sacrifice of individual liberty; that achieving meritocracy will create divisive status inequality; that meritocracy both requires and condemns income inequality and is hence an incoherent ideal; and that meritocracy unfairly disadvantages those who are naturally less gifted than others.

3.1 Why meritocracy?

Gordon Marshall and Adam Swift argue that meritocracy attracts us for two reasons: because it seems efficient and because it seems just (Marshall and Swift, 1997, pp. 42–5).

Let's start with efficiency. Certainly in the case of jobs, if we do not follow the merit principle and allocate jobs to those who are best qualified to do them, then the jobs will be performed more poorly than they need be. Not only are the talented individuals who are squeezed out of the jobs for which they are best qualified injured by this, but so, obviously, is the wider community. Even those who benefit from getting a job for which they are not the best qualified candidate may lose out on balance if many jobs in society are performed by similarly underqualified people.

However, meritocracy seems not only efficient, but just. Many of us have the sense that when two candidates are competing for a job, it is just that the most qualified candidate (qualified in the sense of having those characteristics best suited to doing the job well) be selected. Typically, we say that the most qualified candidate is *deserving* of the job, and that it is unjust if he or she fails to get what he or she deserves. Those sympathetic to meritocracy typically extend this notion of desert to cover the distribution of income as well as the allocation of jobs. As David Miller puts it: 'The merit principle seems to have a firm grounding in popular thinking about justice: it corresponds to the widespread belief that people deserve to enjoy unequal incomes depending on their abilities and how hard they work' (Miller, 2000a, p. 178).

To clarify what is being said here, consider an example. Imagine that a football club employs a group of players, most of whom are rather mediocre, and one of whom is akin to David Beckham. The Beckham-type player contributes more to the team's victories and to the supporters' enjoyment of each match. Aware of his special contribution, the Beckham-type player demands a higher wage for his services than that paid to the other players. Many people would accept that, to some extent, the Beckham-type player deserves the higher pay he demands, by virtue of the special contribution he makes to the team and the quality of the matches they play. They would think it unjust, moreover, to deny this player what he specially deserves.

To be clear, the argument here is not that Beckham-type footballers and other talented workers should be paid more for incentives reasons, because otherwise they will work less or not deploy their special talents at all. That claim might indeed be true, and might give us an additional reason for paying talented workers more than others. (We will consider this incentives argument for inequality in chapter 5.) But the argument I have just described is that, irrespective of the effect of varying pay on the work incentives of the talented, talented workers ought to get higher pay because their superior performances as workers means that they deserve it. Thus, while meritocracy entails a form of equality of opportunity, it emphatically does not require equality of outcome (that is, equality of incomes or wealth). For the meritocrat, maintaining equality of outcome would be unjust because it would entail a failure to give some workers the higher incomes they supposedly deserve.

I have said that meritocracy draws its appeal from the values of efficiency and justice. It looks particularly compelling because it promises to combine them. However, we should note that it is perfectly possible for these two values to come apart. For example, imagine that choosing the most deserving candidate for a job is very costly. The costs are in fact so high that they outweigh the economic benefit to employers and consumers of choosing the best candidate rather than randomly choosing one of a large number of candidates who are all at least tolerably competent. In this case, the value of efficiency will call for a relaxation of the strict application of meritocratic norms. But justice, understood in terms of desert, will oppose this. In this sort of case, society in effect has to pay a price for meritocratic justice: it has to accept a net cost that it could avoid by being less just in this sense.

3.2 Weak meritocracy

Marshall and Swift also helpfully draw attention to important differences in the way the notions of meritocracy and equality of opportunity are understood (Marshall and Swift, 1997, pp. 38–42). It is important to distinguish two very different conceptions of what a meritocracy is, and of the kind of equality of opportunity that a meritocracy entails. The first is what we may call the *weak conception of meritocracy* (or, more simply, weak meritocracy). We may refer to the second, correspondingly, as the *strong conception of meritocracy* (or, more simply, strong meritocracy). The difference between the two has to do with the range of disadvantages that they respectively identify as obstructing equality of opportunity and thereby preventing a truly merit-based distribution of jobs and incomes.

In the case of weak meritocracy, the focus is primarily on one specific source of disadvantage: discrimination, whether by the state and public bodies or by parties in the private sector. The demand for equality of opportunity is understood as consisting in the absence of discrimination in access to important goods such as education and employment. Discrimination is a complex notion, but as a first approximation we can say that it consists in selecting against candidates for jobs and other positions on grounds that are unrelated to their capacity to perform well in the relevant job or position. An example (of racial discrimination) would be an employer choosing a white candidate for a job over a black candidate, even though the black candidate has better qualifications.

One possible source of discrimination is the state itself. Imagine a society in which the law prohibits women from entering the medical profession, and prohibits people of certain religions from going to major universities which offer access to leading positions in society. The first restriction prevents women who have the potential to be excellent doctors from entering the field, which may mean that some posts are taken by less talented men. The second restriction puts members of the affected religions at a severe disadvantage in working their way into elite sections of society and, again, this might result in less able people holding elite positions. A first requirement of weak meritocracy is that the state itself refrain from discrimination of this kind. The demand for 'equality of opportunity' is, in the first instance, the demand for an end to this kind of direct blockage of opportunity by the state.

Even if the state itself does not discriminate, however, parties in the private sector might do so. Employers and private educational institutions might decide on their own initiative to discriminate on grounds of (say) race, gender or religion. This, too, will mean that in some cases the people who are best qualified for a given position will not get it, frustrating the merit principle. To prevent this, many supporters of the ideal of weak meritocracy argue that the state must not only refrain from discrimination itself, but must also intervene to prohibit discrimination by other parties, such as employers and major educational institutions. It must enact a range of anti-discrimination laws that threaten employers and the like with sanctions if they make employment and related decisions on the basis of characteristics such as race, ethnicity, gender, religion or sexual orientation, rather than on the basis of the characteristics that are relevant for the position in question.[1]

It is important to note, however, that the commitment to anti-discrimination legislation does not necessarily follow from the ideal of weak meritocracy in itself. To reach the conclusion that anti-discrimination legislation is necessary to secure weak meritocracy one must first reject the possibility that discrimination will somehow disappear of its own accord without the need for legislation. Some critics of anti-discrimination laws take this view (Sowell, 1981). They argue that if employers do discriminate, they will simply end up with less able workforces than more open-minded employers, and will go under due to this competitive disadvantage. Realizing this, rational employers will, over time, refrain from discrimination of their own accord, making it unnecessary for the state to ban discrimination.

Supporters of anti-discrimination laws make two powerful rejoinders to this argument (Sunstein, 1991). First, they point out that people buying from firms in a given industry might themselves have prejudices that put non-discriminatory employers at a competitive disadvantage. For example, if most white people in a town prefer to be served in a restaurant by white waiters and waitresses, rather than by blacks, then a restaurant which practises non-discrimination between blacks and whites when choosing its staff will get less custom and so may go under, while discriminatory restaurants will flourish. In such a case, anti-discrimination laws seem essential to prevent discrimination.[2] Second, supporters of anti-discrimination laws point to what economists call 'statistical discrimination'. For example, perhaps a given kind of job requires a degree of physical strength which men on average have, but women on average do not. While a particular employer might be well aware that there are some women who could do this job, he/she might choose purely for commercial reasons only to employ men. The reason for this has to do with a point we noted above: that it can be costly in terms of time, labour and other resources to try to pick the best candidate from an applicant pool. In the case we are considering, suppose it is costly to screen job applicants on an individual basis to see whether they have the strength required for the job. By not screening, the employer will end up employing some men who are less able for the job than some women might be. But it is perfectly rational for the employer to bear the costs that result from this if the cost of identifying more talented women in the applicant pool is even higher. Once again, because discrimination in this situation is rational for the employer, legislation seems essential to prevent it.[3]

3.3 Strong meritocracy

Imagine a society in which discrimination has been effectively prevented. However, some children grow up with only a few years of poor schooling because this is all their parents can afford, while other children have parents able to buy them many years of high-quality schooling. Some children inherit large sums from their parents, while others receive no inheritance at all. Is this society a meritocracy? Does it offer its members equality of opportunity? Many supporters of the ideal of meritocracy would argue that this society is not genuinely meritocratic. Even if the absence of discrimination means that jobs (and incomes) do go to those who, in an immediate sense, are best qualified and so most merit them, background inequalities, such as those in education and financial inheritance, mean that some people are seriously disadvantaged compared with others in their opportunities to develop their talents and to apply them for reward. Thus, there is not real equality of opportunity, and people who have a lot of latent merit might not be able to shine through.

This insight underpins the perspective I term strong meritocracy. Strong meritocracy endorses the aims of weak meritocracy, but adds to them a concern with the environment in which individuals grow up, and with the initial resources on which they have to draw. The rationale for strong meritocracy, in preference to weak meritocracy, is one of both efficiency and justice. A weak meritocracy could be inefficient relative to a strong meritocracy because its failure to tackle inequalities in opportunity to develop and apply talent, other than those caused by discrimination, will leave some of society's native talent underused. The British politician Tony Crosland put the point as follows:

> Clever working-class children are still denied access to the public schools, while the less clever but still potentially useful have only a rather uncertain access to the grammar schools; and there is certainly no perfect correspondence between natural talent and type of education. Moreover . . . inherited property, nepotism, and class favouritism all prevent a fair and effective competition, on merit alone, for the highest posts.
>
> It follows that we are still not extracting the best from our population, or making the most exhaustive use of scarce resources of human ability. (Crosland, 1956, p. 147)[4]

Moreover, because weak meritocracy does not tackle inequalities in opportunity such as those due to disadvantages in education and inheritance, it seems less fair or just than strong meritocracy. It leaves each person's prospects in life radically dependent on accident of birth and this, in itself, seems unjust. Bernard Williams explains the point as follows:

> Suppose that in a certain society great prestige is attached to membership of a warrior class, the duties of which require great physical strength. This class has in the past been recruited from certain wealthy families only; but egalitarian reformers achieve a change in the rules, by which warriors are recruited from all sections of the society, on the results of a suitable competition. The effect of this, however, is that the wealthy families still provide virtually all the warriors, because the rest of the populace is so under-nourished by reason of poverty that their physical strength is inferior to that of the wealthy and well-nourished. The reformers protest that equality of opportunity has not really been achieved; the wealthy reply that in fact it has, that the poor now have the opportunity of becoming warriors – it is just bad luck that their characteristics are such that they do not pass the test. 'We are not,' they might say, 'excluding anyone *for* being poor; we exclude people for being weak, and it is unfortunate that those who are poor are also weak.'
>
> This answer would seem to most people feeble, and even cynical. (Williams, 1973, pp. 244–5)

In addition to discrimination, then, strong meritocrats believe that we need to attend to disadvantage in at least three other areas: (1) inherited wealth; (2) education; (3) family environment.

In countries like Britain and the United States there are considerable inequalities in the wealth that individuals receive through gift and inheritance from friends and family members (Rowlingson and McKay, 2005; Paxton and Dixon, 2005, p. 54). This matters, in the view of the strong meritocrat, because the wealth that individuals have at their disposal at the start of their working lives can have a major effect on their success in later life. People who inherit a substantial amount in their early adult years have more ability to step back from earning a living for a while to think about what they wish to do with their lives. They are likely to find it easier to get credit as they can offer some of their wealth as collateral (Hoff, 1998). They can use their wealth as a cushion to undertake risky, but potentially very rewarding, ventures. One recent study finds, for example, that individuals who receive an inheritance are more likely to set up their own businesses (Blanchflower and Oswald, 1998), and there is a much larger body of evidence which finds correlations between the assets people have and a range of life-outcomes, including physical and psychological health, probability of employment, civic involvement, and children's educational attainment (for an overview, see Paxton, 2001; for a more sceptical view on the existence of some of these 'asset effects', see also McKay and Kempson, 2003). Given these findings, it is also not surprising to find that differences in the wealth that people inherit or receive through gifts seem to explain a significant proportion of overall inequality of wealth, though estimates of the exact proportion vary (see Keister, 2000, pp. 252–6). The implication is that if we desire equality of opportunity, then inequalities in inherited wealth must be moderated. One proposal, which goes back at least as far as Tom Paine (Paine, 1987 [1797]), is to tax estates or wealth transfers and to use the funds to finance a system of capital grants for all – a kind of *citizens' inheritance* (Haveman, 1988; Ackerman and Alstott, 1999; Nissan and Le Grand, 2000; Paxton et al., 2006). In Paine's proposal, each individual would get a sum of capital on maturity:

When a young couple begin the world the difference is exceed-
ingly great whether they begin the world with nothing or with
fifteen pounds apiece. With this aid they could buy a cow, and
implements to cultivate a few acres of land; and instead of
becoming burdens upon society . . . would be put in the way
of becoming useful and profitable citizens. (Paine, 1987
[1797], p. 483)

A second area of concern for strong meritocrats is that of
education. For equality of opportunity it is necessary to structure education systems so that children with the same ability
and motivation – let us say the same 'potential' – have equal
prospects of developing their ability, of realizing their potential. One child should not have lower prospects than another
because they have been born into a lower social class (or, say,
because they are female or belong to a particular ethnic
group).[5] How to achieve this objective is the subject of intense
debate amongst educationalists. In general, strong meritocrats have supported efforts to reduce the power of parents
from higher social classes to segregate their children in better
schools. This has involved discouraging private education,
discouraging too much selection and streaming within the
state sector, and trying to ensure parity of resources across
state schools (Crosland, 1956, pp. 258–77; Esping-Andersen,
2005, p. 32).

For many years, strong meritocrats pinned a lot of hope
on reforms to the education system. But research suggests
that, despite efforts at educational reform, equality of opportunity may not have increased that much (Esping-Andersen,
2005, p. 33, citing Erikson and Goldthorpe, 1992; Shavit and
Bossfeld, 1993). This might be because of a third factor that
is of concern to the strong meritocrat: the family environment. The kind of nutrition, support and stimulation children
receive from their parents, especially in their early years, can
have a major impact on the development of basic personal
capacities, including the cognitive capacities, motivation and
social skills needed to make good progress in school and in
employment. One recent British study shows that by the age
of twenty-two months children's average scores on cognitive
tests already differ strikingly by the social class of their
parents (Feinstein, 2003). This might reflect differences in

resources between families. But there could be other factors at work that affect children's intellectual development as they grow up, related to differences in parenting styles and 'cultural capital'. One recent study by Annette Lareau in the United States looks intensively at parenting styles in middle-class, working-class and poor families (Lareau, 2003). Lareau finds that middle-class parents adopt a style of 'concerted cultivation' which involves many 'organized activities' for their children, with interaction characterized by a lot of talk and with a strong emphasis on persuasion rather than direction. In contrast, working-class and poor parents tend to see parenting in terms of the 'accomplishment of natural growth'. The task of parenting is understood in terms of ensuring children's material well-being and safety while leaving them, within these parameters, free to pursue their own goals. Interactions between parents and children tend to be less conversational and more directive. Both parenting styles have their advantages and disadvantages, but Lareau argues that the middle-class style tends to generate skills and expectations that serve children better in education and employment. In another recent study, using data from a range of affluent nations, Gøsta Esping-Andersen has examined how children's cognitive performance at age fifteen is affected by parental income, education and 'culture', where culture is measured in terms of 'the quantity of books in the home, the frequency of discussing cultural issues, and . . . frequency of attending concerts, theatre, etc.' He finds that this cultural variable explains more of the difference in children's cognitive performances than income or socioeconomic status (Esping-Andersen, 2005, p. 33). The family environment might also be very important in affecting equality of opportunity between the sexes. For example, if parents teach their children that a 'woman's place is in the home', then this might discourage girls from trying hard or studying certain subjects at school. The strong meritocrat will be concerned, then, to find ways of combating the differential effects of family environment on children's development of cognitive abilities, social skills and motivation.

Clearly, strong meritocracy is a much more demanding political ideal than weak meritocracy. Indeed, unless we are willing to abolish the family, it is almost certainly impossible to achieve it to a full extent. However, just because an ideal is not fully attainable this does not mean that we should not try to achieve it so far as we can.

3.4 How meritocratic is contemporary society?

To what extent is our society actually meritocratic? Is a society like Britain today close to equality of opportunity?

To address this question, sociologists examine the rate of mobility across social classes (*social mobility*).[6] In studies of this kind, social class is frequently defined in terms of broad occupational groups. Following John Goldthorpe (Goldthorpe, 1980), many researchers employ a six- or seven-class model consisting of: class I, higher salariat (professionals and managers of large business concerns); class II, lower salariat (semi-professional workers, managers and administrators in small businesses); class III, routine white-collar workers; class IV, traditional petite bourgeoisie (farmers, small employers, the self-employed); classes V and VI, higher working class (skilled manual workers); class VII, lower working class (semi-skilled and unskilled manual workers).[7] The studies then use data collected from social surveys to explore how the class position of respondents compares with that of the respondents' parents. If the respondent is in a higher social class than his or her parents, then he or she has experienced upward social mobility. If the respondent is in a lower social class than his or her parents, then he or she has experienced downward social mobility. By looking at patterns of social mobility, and at information on the determinants of individuals' class positions, we can begin to get a picture of how meritocratic our society is.

Assume we are interested in whether Britain is meritocratic in the strong sense. If society were meritocratic in this sense, with real equality of opportunity, then we might expect to see a significant degree of upward social mobility out of the working class (classes V, VI and VII) into the intermediate classes (classes III and IV) and the salariat (classes I and II). Table 3.1 below reports the results of a 1991 survey of how the class position of sons born in 1958 compares with that of their fathers. If one looks at the third column of the table one sees that about 45 per cent of sons born in 1958 who had working-class fathers had, by 1991, moved into occupations in the intermediate class and the salariat. This seems to indicate quite a high level of upward social mobility, and so we might be tempted to conclude that Britain is meritocratic.

However, this conclusion is too hasty. To see why, let's take another look at table 3.1. Looking at the first row of the table, we see that sons born to salariat fathers in 1958 had a 61 per cent chance of ending up in the salariat in 1991, as compared with a 26 per cent chance for sons born in the same year to working-class fathers. In other words, the odds of a salariat son entering the salariat are more than twice those of a working-class son (61/26 = 2.35). Looking now at the third row of the table, we see that sons born to salariat fathers had an 18 per cent chance of entering the working class, whereas sons born to working-class fathers had a 55 per cent chance of ending up in the working class. Thus, the odds of a salariat son ending up in the working class are around one-third of those of a son born into the working class (18/55 = 0.327). So the chances of ending up in one class position rather than another do seem to be affected by one's class of origin: people born into a higher social class are more likely to be in it as adults than those born into a lower social class (and vice versa for those born into the lower social classes).[8] Does this not show a lack of equality of opportunity and, hence, the absence of meritocracy?

Table 3.1 The class destinations of sons born in 1958 (Britain)

	Class of father			
	Salariat	Intermediate	Working class	Total
Class of son				
Salariat	61%	40%	26%	36%
Intermediate	20%	26%	19%	21%
Working class	18%	34%	55%	43%

Source: Roberts, 2001, p. 197, adapted from Savage and Egerton, 1997.

It might well do. But we have to be careful about rushing to a conclusion on the basis of this kind of information alone (Marshall, Swift and Roberts, 1997). What is indisputable here is that sons born to high-class positions have a much higher statistical chance of ending up in these positions than sons born to lower-class positions, and a much lower statistical chance of ending up in lower-class positions than sons born into lower-class positions. One explanation of this finding is that there is unequal opportunity in British society due to things like discrimination, the structure of the education system, and the distribution of inherited wealth. However, as Gordon Marshall and his colleagues stress in a recent study, there are other possible explanations for the finding (Marshall, Swift and Roberts, 1997). One is that the children born to working-class parents simply have *less natural ability* than those born to higher-class parents. They do not, according to this hypothesis, suffer less opportunity to develop and deploy their abilities, but are endowed by nature, on average, with less ability, e.g., lower intelligence, and this explains why they have less chance of ending up in higher-class positions. A second possibility is that the children born to working-class parents have *less motivation* than those born to higher-class parents. According to this hypothesis, they do not have less opportunity to reach any given class position, but they are less interested in getting to the higher positions.

The sociologist Peter Saunders argues that these two factors are in fact the important ones in explaining the observed differences in social mobility rates (Saunders, 1995). Saunders examines how the class position of individuals in later life relates to their scores in intelligence tests taken as eleven-year-olds (Intelligent Quotient or IQ). He finds a strong association between class position in later life and childhood IQ, and argues that this supports the theory that inequalities in class position in later life reflect differences in natural ability. Saunders also finds that, after childhood IQ scores, a measure of motivation in childhood is the second best single predictor of individuals' class positions in adult life. The observed differences in social mobility are, on this view, much more a reflection of inequalities in ability and motivation than in opportunity, and so do not discredit the idea that Britain is a meritocracy.

However, there are big problems with Saunders's argument. First, it is very questionable whether measured IQ at age eleven is a good measure of children's raw ability. By this age, children's cognitive abilities might already have been powerfully influenced by factors associated with their social class and family environment (Marshall, Swift and Roberts, 1997, pp. 141–4).[9] One recent study that we noted above, by Leon Feinstein, tracks how children from different social classes perform on cognitive tests as they get older. It shows that children from low classes who perform very well on these tests at twenty-two months are gradually caught up and overtaken around age seven by children from higher social classes who initially perform less well on the tests (Feinstein, 2003). Initially 'smarter' children in lower-class backgrounds slowly lose this advantage as they get older, indicating that children's intellectual development could well be affected by their class and/or family environment long before they reach eleven. Second, the distinction that Saunders makes between motivation and opportunity as factors in explaining differences in social mobility is a problematic one. Surely one way in which a person's opportunity in life can be diminished is by growing up in a social environment which undermines or dampens down her motivation. If a child with high latent ability is born into a family that discourages educational effort, then can we not say that this family environment in itself constitutes an obstacle to her opportunity? This is not to say that all motivational differences represent restrictions on equality of opportunity or are morally objectionable (see Marshall, Swift and Roberts, 1997, pp. 139–41; Swift, 2003, 2004).[10] But some of them are, and Saunders does not seem to take this into account.

In short, the evidence we have to hand does not allow us to say conclusively how far differences in relative mobility rates between people born into different social classes do reflect unequal opportunities. It would be surprising, however, if all of the difference in mobility rates could be explained by other factors. The most recent and comprehensive study of this topic in the United States argues that there is still a lot we don't understand about the mechanisms which limit social mobility, but it also concludes that we do know that genetics, environment and wealth all play a role (Bowles,

Gintis, and Osborne Groves, 2005, pp. 1–22). The thesis that British society is a long way from being a strong meritocracy is, therefore, a reasonable one.

Britain has an image as a particularly class-bound society in which social position is strongly influenced by the position of one's parents (after all, the position of head of state is a hereditary one). So perhaps Britain is distinctive in apparently being unmeritocratic? Comparative research on social mobility suggests not. In virtually all economically developed nations we see a strong statistical relationship between an individual's class of origin and class of destination, a relationship which has not diminished notably over time (Erikson and Goldthorpe, 1992; Shavit and Bossfeld, 1993); the only partial exceptions to this are the Scandinavian countries, where class inheritance does seem to have diminished somewhat in recent years (Esping-Andersen, 2005).[11]

3.5   Against meritocracy 1: threat to liberty

Is meritocracy (weak or strong) really that desirable? Is this the ideal that citizens in a moralized democracy should hold before them when they try to make laws that will treat each citizen fairly? In this and the following two sections we will look at some important arguments against meritocracy. A first criticism is that even if meritocracy is desirable in principle, we should limit our action to promote it out of respect for personal freedom.

Imagine that people who are involved in a line of business or a profession form a club or dining society. They are selective as to whom they will let in, refusing, say, to admit women. This exclusion then puts women at a disadvantage in the business or profession in question. Lacking access to the club, they do not have the same opportunity to network with possible collaborators, colleagues and employers. People who belong to such associations might also become more knowledgeable about and sympathetic to fellow insiders, so biasing them against outsiders in subtle, perhaps unconscious, ways when they are making hiring and promotion decisions. The exclusion from the club clearly compromises women's equality of opportunity with men. It gets in the way of meritocracy. But some argue that freedom of association is a basic personal liberty which would be violated if, for the sake of meritocracy, the state were to prohibit private associations to practise exclusion of this kind.

Other objections of this kind abound. For example, how can a society ensure that children get equal educational opportunity unless it prohibits aspirational parents from using their resources in ways that secure superior educational opportunities for their children, e.g., by paying fees for private schools or simply hiring private tutors to supplement teaching at school? How can a society prevent inequality in wealth inheritances unless it removes the freedom of parents and other relatives to transmit wealth to their offspring? To the extent that the state can combat things like a lack of cultural capital within families, is this not likely to involve a massive degree of intrusion into family life? If, say, the state tries directly to combat the efforts of parents to socialize their children into traditional gender roles, will it not find itself quickly in conflict with parents belonging to various faith groups, such as some fundamentalist Christians, who support these gender roles? What, then, of the value of freedom of religion? Putting all these objections together, the critic will argue that we can have either a meritocratic society or a free society, and that we should choose a free society (Hayek, 1960). Here I note just two ways in which a supporter of action to promote meritocracy can respond to this freedom-based challenge.

First, in some cases, the meritocrat can respond that what promotes equality of opportunity also promotes personal freedom, properly understood. Let us go back to the case of the fundamentalist parents who wish to raise their daughters in the belief that a woman's place is in the home. It is not a question, in such a case, of the state acting to ensure that these girls grow up to believe the opposite of what their parents believe. Rather, it is a question of ensuring that they grow up with the capacity to assess their parents' views – and rival views – in a reasoned and informed manner, so that they can make their own choice about whether or not they wish to be housewives. In the language of contemporary political philosophy, it is a question of ensuring that these girls have 'autonomy': the capacity to reflect and make one's own informed decisions about how to live. But this autonomy is itself a very important kind of personal freedom. In acting to protect equality of opportunity in this case, then, the state is not necessarily acting for 'equality' against 'liberty'. It is acting to promote one kind of liberty over another kind: children's freedom to choose their own way of life when mature is being promoted over the freedom of their parents to bring children up in a way that ties them into their faith community. It is by no means obvious that we should value the parental freedom in play here more than the children's freedom.

Second, the meritocrat can argue that it is sometimes possible to go quite a long way in reducing inequality of opportunity before important personal freedoms are threatened. Consider, for example, the objection that taxation of inheritances will infringe the freedom of parents and other relatives to pass wealth on to descendants. We can agree that allowing people *some* freedom of this kind is important because the transfer of wealth between family members is an important means of expressing familial affection. But these interests can arguably be satisfied by allowing every citizen a modest 'lifetime accessions quota': a quota of wealth that they may receive via inheritance, bequest or gift over the course of their whole lifetime without any liability to tax. Tax can then apply to all wealth transfers over this modest threshold (Meade, 1964). This type of tax regime will help to limit inequality in initial endowments of wealth, while still giving family members some freedom to transfer certain items of emotional significance across the generations.

Similarly, in the case of freedom of association, the government need not choose between banning all exclusion from private associations by gender or race on the one hand, and permitting all such exclusion on the other. In the United States, the Supreme Court has developed a much more nuanced approach which allows the government to take action against exclusion from clubs and associations in many contexts, but which also protects the most important kinds of freedom of association (White, 1997). The issue came to prominence in the 1980s in a court case, Roberts *vs.* Jaycees. The case concerned whether a state government could force the local branch of the 'Jaycees', a national organization for young businessmen, to admit women as full members. The Supreme Court judged that the state was not acting in violation of the United States Constitution when it required the Jaycees to do this. The Court argued that there are two fundamental freedoms of association that warrant constitutional protection: firstly, freedom of intimate association, the kind of association typified by forming a family or arranging a night out with friends; and, secondly, freedom of expressive association, the kind of association typified by religious and political associations that have a belief system to express and pursue. But the Court reasoned that in this case neither freedom was threatened by the requirement that the Jaycees admit women as full members. With a national mass-membership, the Jaycees clearly were not an intimate association. And, while the Jaycees did take a stand on some public issues, the organization could not show that a rule excluding women from full membership was necessary to protect its distinctive campaigning position. Thus, the Court concluded, the state could require the Jaycees to change its membership policy if it had reason to think this would promote equality of opportunity.

In short, while liberty-based objections to action that establishes meritocracy ought not to be dismissed, and may sometimes be valid, there is much that the meritocrat can say in reply to such objections. In this context, as more generally, we need to dig down beneath the abstract slogans of 'liberty' and 'equality' in order to consider the concrete interests that are at stake in each type of case.

3.6 Against meritocracy 2: status inequality

The term 'meritocracy' was popularized by Michael Young's influential book, *The Rise of the Meritocracy* (Young, 1958).[12] In this book, Young warns that as a society advances towards strong meritocracy, this could come at the price of status equality. The danger arises firstly because in a strong meritocracy the people who end up in lower social classes cannot explain their lowliness away on a lack of opportunity. They are presumably where they are in the social scale because they do not have the ability to be higher up. This may lead to a sense of genuine inferiority on their part. In writing the book, Young pretends to be a graduate student of the 2030s looking back on the development of meritocracy in Britain, and his student narrator puts the point as follows:

> Today all persons, however humble, know they have had every chance. . . . If they have been labelled 'dunce' repeatedly they cannot any longer pretend. . . . Are they not bound to recognize that they have inferior status – not as in the past because they were denied opportunity, but because they *are* inferior? (Young, 1958, pp. 86–7)

At the same time, people in higher social classes know they are there because they do have high ability. This may create a sense of superiority on their part. As Young's narrator describes the situation:

> Hence one of the characteristic modern problems – some members of the meritocracy . . . have become so impressed with their own importance as to lose sympathy with the people whom they govern, and so tactless that even people of low calibre have been quite unnecessarily offended. (p. 86)

Is there a way to handle this threat to status equality? David Miller, a qualified supporter of meritocracy, suggests two ways of tackling the problem. First, he argues, it is important to 'offset' the meritocratic distribution of jobs and incomes by cultivating a 'robust form of equal citizenship' (Miller, 2000a, p. 200). The government must act so that people develop a 'strong understanding of their equality as citizens regardless of their economic deserts'. How might this be done? Miller suggests that some social goods, such as health care, should be taken out of the realm of the market-place, and provided on a public basis for all citizens on a basis of equality. Another suggestion is to require all youths to participate in a national service scheme (with non-military options like environmental work or service in schools). As one advocate, Mickey Kaus, puts it: 'For social egalitarians . . . national service is valuable precisely because it would force [people] to pause in their disparate career trajectories and immerse themselves in a common, public enterprise' (Kaus, 1992, p. 81). People from different backgrounds would rub shoulders with one another in shared projects and this 'class-mixing' might enhance fellowship and respect for others as equals.

Second, Miller argues that society needs to explicitly distinguish between economic merit or desert and merit in a wider, comprehensive sense. There are lots of grounds for respecting people and according them esteem. One is economic success. But others include: sporting prowess, intellectual achievement, being a good parent, acting as a pillar of the neighbourhood and so on. Society needs to find ways of acknowledging all these different kinds of merit. If it succeeds, then it is possible that one person's merit in one area will be matched by another's merit in a different area, and an overall hierarchy of esteem, based solely on economic merit, will not arise. Status equality is in this way maintained. This is also Michael Young's view:

> The classless society would be one which both possessed and acted upon plural values. Were we to evaluate people, not according to their intelligence and education, their occupation and their power, but according to their kindness and their courage, their imagination and sensitivity, their sympathy and generosity, there would be no classes. Who would be able to say that the scientist was superior to the porter with admirable qualities as a father...? (1958, p. 135)

Do these responses defuse the status inequality objection? Possibly. But to be sure we would have to do some empirical research to gauge how effective they are (for example, into how far national service programmes do encourage status equality). The second response is also a little abstract. How, concretely, can a government promote a pluralist understanding of merit? If income and wealth inequality are salient facts, with important repercussions for people's lives, how can we stop people basing their evaluations of others primarily on their success in the marketplace? In short, these two responses are suggestive, but there is a need for more work on policy development and research into the effects of policy before we can assess whether they are decisive.

3.7 Against meritocracy 3: incoherence

Strong meritocrats support equality of opportunity (in the sense defined in section 3.3), but not equality of outcome, that is, of income and wealth. On the meritocratic view, some inequality of income and wealth is allegedly deserved and it would be unjust to try to eliminate it. However, if we allow inequality of incomes and wealth, will this not tend to undermine equality of opportunity? Some children will grow up in families that are much better off than others and this might give them an advantage in developing their skills and ambitions. To maintain equality of opportunity, therefore, do we not have to sustain a high level of equality of outcome? As the sociologist Fred Hirsch puts it: 'At the limit, the criterion of an equal start is an equal finish' (Hirsch, 1977, p. 5). Some empirical support for this view is provided by the Scandinavian countries which show, in relative terms, both low levels of income inequality and high rates of social mobility (Esping-Andersen, 2005). If outcome equality is necessary for equality of opportunity, however, then in any society with multiple generations, the ideal of strong meritocracy looks incoherent: apparently, it simultaneously demands that we tolerate inequality of outcome and that we do not tolerate it.

This criticism certainly points to a genuine tension within the ideal of strong meritocracy. But whether the tension implies full-blown incoherence is less clear. The key question is this: Is there some level of income and wealth inequality which is high enough to acknowledge the (alleged) special deserts of some workers, but not so high as to seriously compromise equal opportunity for the next generation? If there is, then strong meritocracy is coherent as an ideal. We cannot say as a philosophical matter whether there is such a level of income or wealth inequality; finding the answer will require careful empirical research. One further point to make, in support of the strong meritocrat, is that he or she is not committed to the idea that economic desert ought to govern fully the distribution of all goods (Miller, 2000a, p. 200). Quite the opposite. He or she will want many of the most important social goods – education, health care, to some extent inheritances of wealth – to be taken out of the market sphere and provided to all on the basis of equality. The strong meritocrat will want this partly to foster real equality of opportunity and partly to promote the strong sense of equal citizenship referred to above. When all of these initiatives are added together, some inequality in incomes and wealth will remain, but it is an open question as to how far these residual inequalities will undermine equality of opportunity given the range of goods that people will have access to independently of their (or their parents') income and wealth.

However, even if this residual inequality of income and wealth is consistent with equality of opportunity, perhaps it is in itself unjust? This question brings us to our final criticism of meritocracy.

3.8 Against meritocracy 4: unfair to the less talented

Meritocrats believe that if there is sufficient equality of opportunity, then resulting inequalities in earnings between workers with different levels of skill are just. They claim that more skilled workers deserve a good portion of the higher earnings they get. Why do the more talented deserve (at least some of) the higher pay they get? The usual answer is: because, if they employ their skills, they contribute more to society than other workers. This greater contribution deserves to be rewarded. To many people, this seems obvious.

But is it really so obvious? Imagine two people, John and Joanne. John's abilities (over which he has no control) are such that, working at his best, he can produce a service that is worth £15,000 a year to society. Joanne has abilities such that, working to her best, she can produce a service worth £150,000 a year. John decides to work at his best, producing a benefit to society of £15,000 in a given year, while Joanne decides to take things easy and produce goods worth £30,000 in a given year. Now Joanne has made twice the contribution that John has. So does she have double the economic merit or desert of John? Is she even *more* deserving than he? Given the facts, it is far from obvious that she is. After all, John has worked to his very best, while Joanne has worked well below her best. Viewed in this light, is it not plausible to say that John is the more deserving of the two? Perhaps our assessment of an individual's deservingness should depend not (or not only) on the *absolute* value of what they produce for others, but (also) on the value of what they produce *relative to their personal capacity to produce*. An analogy might be made with our intuitions in the case of charitable giving. If a poor person gives, say, £5 to a charity, many people would judge this action as more meritorious, in a moral sense, than a very rich person's giving £5, or even £50, to charity. Why does a similar logic not apply to economic production?

The implication of this alternative view is that one worker does not deserve a lower reward than others because she is endowed by nature (or by social factors beyond her control) with inferior productive abilities. In principle, according to this view, incomes for work should differ only to reflect the different choices people make as to how far to exercise the talents they are endowed with (White, 1999).[13]

Moreover, this shift in perspective can also be seen as developing further another core idea of meritocracy, that of equality of opportunity. The weak meritocrat, as we have seen, identifies equality of opportunity with the absence of discrimination. The strong meritocrat argues that, by itself, this will not really secure equality of opportunity because even in the absence of discrimination some people can end up with significantly worse prospects than others due to differences in class and family background that affect such things as their educational opportunities and their inheritance of wealth. It is unjust, according to the strong meritocrat, that 'accidents of birth' like this can exert such a major influence on people's prospects. But our natural endowments, which affect our intelligence and a whole range of skills, are also determined by accident of birth. So if we think justice requires us to tackle inequalities in prospects due to one set of accidents of birth (very roughly, class-based inheritances), does justice not also require us to mitigate the inequality due to this other (nature-based) kind of accident of birth? 'There is,' the philosopher John Rawls argues, 'no more reason to permit the distribution of income and wealth to be settled by the distribution of natural assets than by historical and social fortune' (Rawls, 1999a, p. 64). Anticipating Rawls, the sociologist, Émile Durkheim, put the point well in his lectures on 'civic morals':

> To us it does not seem equitable that a man should be better treated as a social being because he was born of parentage that is rich or of high rank. But is it any more equitable that he should be better treated because he was born of a father of higher intelligence...? (Durkheim, 1957, p. 220)

Echoing Rawls and Durkheim, Ronald Dworkin claims that the meritocratic conception of equality of opportunity, even in its strong form, is 'fraudulent'. It frustrates real equality of opportunity because it leaves people's prospects at the mercy of natural endowments over which they have no control (Dworkin, 1985; see also Barry, 2005). But if we accept this argument, as I think we must, where does it lead? What is the alternative to meritocracy, weak or strong?

4
Luck Egalitarianism

The wise and patient workman strikes his spade in here, and with heavy toil can discover nothing but a poor quality of barley, some potatoes and plentiful nettles, with a few dock leaves to cure his stings. The foolish spendthrift on the other side of the hedge, gazing idly at the sand glittering in the sun, suddenly realizes that the earth is offering him gold – is dancing it before his listless eyes lest it should escape him. . . . Thus is Man mocked by Earth, his step-mother, and never knows as he tugs at her closed hand whether it contains diamonds or flints, good red wheat or a few clayey and blighted cabbages.

George Bernard Shaw, *Fabian Essays in Socialism*, 1889

In their search for economic arrangements that treat all members of society fairly, the citizens of a moralized democracy have good reason to question the ideal of meritocracy. An alternative ideal they might consider to guide their deliberations is what Elizabeth Anderson calls *luck egalitarianism* (Anderson, 1999). According to this ideal, inequalities that reflect brute luck, over which people have no control, are unjust, and the community should correct, or act to prevent, such inequalities; but inequalities that reflect the different choices people make, such as choices about how hard to work or whether to take a gamble, are just, and so ought to be respected. Sections 4.1 and 4.2 of this chapter clarify the luck egalitarian ideal. Section 4.1 outlines Ronald Dworkin's theory of 'equality of resources' (which is not at all as simplistic as the label suggests). Section 4.2 considers criticisms, advanced by G. A. Cohen and Amartya Sen, that Dworkin misidentifies the appropriate focus of egalitarian concern in the resources people have to the exclusion of the welfare they enjoy or of what they are more generally able to do and be with resources.

Sections 4.3 and 4.4 then discuss two important objections to luck egalitarianism. Section 4.3 considers an objection from the 'right': that luck egalitarianism demands heavy taxation that is incompatible with respect for personal freedom. It focuses in particular on the charge that taxation of labour incomes violates the worker's rights of self-ownership and thereby reduces the worker to a position relevantly similar to that of a slave. Section 4.4 considers an objection from the 'left': that luck egalitarianism will give rise to objectionable inequalities in power and status, so undermining the goals of political and social equality. A third objection, that rigorous application of luck egalitarianism, or something akin to it, will undermine economic incentives and so impoverish the community, is the focus of chapter 5.

4.1 'Equality of resources'

Ronald Dworkin argues that economic fairness consists in what he calls, perhaps misleadingly, 'equality of resources'. His account of what this means rests on two basic ideas (Dworkin, 2000, pp. 5–7). One is that each person has a special responsibility for the success of her own life. The other is that the political community is obliged to treat its members with equal concern and respect. No one who has a firm sense of her own dignity can tolerate living under rules that intentionally or predictably consign her to more inferior life-chances than others. Putting these two ideas together, Dworkin argues that a fair economic distribution must at once be *ambition-sensitive* and *endowment-insensitive* (Dworkin, 2000, p. 89). Ambition-sensitivity requires that we respect the distributional consequences of the different lifestyle choices people make. We require people to bear the costs of their choices, rather than expecting others to subsidize them. Endowment-insensitivity consists in ensuring that individuals do not have fewer resources than others through no fault of their own. Meritocracy, even in its strong form, is unfair in Dworkin's view because it leaves resource prospects dependent on unequal natural endowments. But note also that his view does not support what we usually mean by equality of outcome: if Smith has more income than Jones because he chooses to work longer hours then the principle of ambition-sensitivity requires that we respect this inequality. In Dworkin's words: 'there is nothing to be said for a world in which those who choose leisure, though they could work, are rewarded with the produce of the industrious' (Dworkin, 2000, p. 2). (This is why, in my view, Dworkin's view is not very helpfully labelled as 'equality of resources'; this label invites confusion with equality of outcome.)

This distinction is related to another distinction that Dworkin makes, between *brute luck* and *option luck* (Dworkin, 2000, pp. 73–4). Something is a matter of brute luck when it is reasonably seen as being beyond the individual's control; if I walk down the street and a meteor hits me out of the blue, this is (bad) brute luck. Option luck, by contrast, is a matter of choosing to expose oneself to certain risks which may then turn out well or badly. If I gamble my life savings on a horse race, then, if the horse loses, I have bad option luck, and if it wins, I have good option luck. Endowment-insensitivity requires that we protect people from resource disadvantage due to bad brute luck. Ambition-sensitivity requires that we respect inequalities that emerge from option luck. If Smith and Jones both start with a million pounds which they gamble, and Smith wins and Jones loses, then the resulting inequality between them is, on the view I am describing, just.

Dworkin's task, then, is to show how an economic distribution can at once be ambition-sensitive and correct for unequal endowments. His discussion falls into two parts, covering what we may call external resources and internal resources. He is also concerned to defend his focus on resources as opposed to welfare. Let us look at each of these aspects of his theory in turn.

1. *External resources.* Imagine a group of people who find themselves shipwrecked on a previously uninhabited island. The island contains various external resources – trees, streams, land and so on. How should these external resources be divided up amongst the newly arrived islanders? In answer to this question, Dworkin introduces the idea of an *initial auction* (Dworkin, 2000, pp. 65–71). Each islander gets an equal share of money (clamshells are used as currency) and is allowed to bid for the resources in the auction. The auction ends when every participant, possessed of equal purchasing power, is satisfied with the resources that she has bought at the prices offered and, at these prices, all resources are sold. Each islander is then entitled to the specific bundle of resources that she has purchased. The resulting distribution does not reflect any inequality of endowments because each islander has the same allocation of money (the clamshells) with which to buy resources. At the same time, the distribution is ambition-sensitive because the specific resources that people have in their bundles will reflect the choices they have individually made about how to spend their endowment of money.

However, now consider two islanders, Anna and Bert. In addition to the resources she has acquired through the auction, Anna is in perfect health and has very productive talents. Bert, by contrast, has a handicap that impairs his mobility, and also has very limited productive talents. While the two are equal in terms of external resources, they are very unequal in their endowments of internal resources: handicaps and productive talents.

2. *Internal resources.* To address this inequality, Dworkin introduces the idea of the *hypothetical insurance market* (Dworkin, 2000, pp. 77–109; see also Kymlicka, 2001, pp.76–9, for a helpful summary). In real life, many of us are able to anticipate potential bad luck by taking out insurance. What if we could also take out insurance against being born with poor internal endowments, e.g., with an immobilizing disability or low earnings capacity? In practice, of course, we can't do this. But imagine that the islanders we have been considering do not yet know what their

individual internal resources are, though they do know what the distribution of internal resources across the population as a whole is like. In this situation, insurance companies could offer the islanders insurance against having poor internal resources, and, using their equal initial shares of wealth (or pledging some share of their future earnings), the islanders could buy insurance against having poor internal resources. In the market itself, they will each have to weigh up whether they want to spend a large portion of their initial wealth and future earnings on an expensive insurance policy that will provide very generous compensation should they turn out to have poor internal resources, or whether they prefer to risk taking out a cheaper, less generous insurance policy.

In practice, of course, it is impossible to say exactly how much insurance each individual would choose to take out. However, Dworkin contends that we can make a realistic assessment of the insurance package that 'the average member of the community [would] purchase' (Dworkin, 2000, pp. 78–9). We can then take this average as a guide for public policy. The government can set transfers and taxes to match the benefits and premium of the average insurance policy. The resulting pattern of transfers will not be perfectly just since some people would have purchased policies below or above the average. But this approach is a reasonable second-best – about as close to justice as we can be expected to get.[1]

3. *Against equality of welfare.* Dworkin puts forward 'equality of resources' as an alternative to another theory, or set of theories, which he terms 'equality of welfare'. This conception of equality, Dworkin says, has an 'immediate appeal' which 'lies in the idea that welfare is what really matters to people, as distinct from money and goods' (Dworkin, 2000, p. 31). According to the 'success' view of welfare, welfare is a matter of how successful someone is in realizing their goals and projects. According to the 'conscious state' or 'hedonic' view, welfare is the amount of enjoyment someone has in life. Depending on which view of welfare one accepts, equality of welfare holds that government should distribute resources so as to achieve equality in how successfully people realize their goals or in how happy they are (Dworkin, 2000, pp. 28–42).

Dworkin identifies a number of problems for equality of welfare. For example, imagine that we have a situation of equality in both resources and welfare. Someone – Dworkin calls him Louis – now decides to cultivate new tastes that are expensive to satisfy, such as tastes for 'plovers' eggs and pre-phyloxera claret' (Dworkin, 2000, p. 49). To maintain equality of welfare, we will have to change the distribution of resources, giving the person who has developed the expensive tastes more resources and others fewer. But why should the others have fewer resources because one person decides to develop more costly tastes? Or consider someone who has a serious mobility handicap, but who nevertheless has equal welfare to others because he has learned to be stoical and make the most of his endowments. Do we not think that such a person should receive some assistance to deal with his handicap, even though he does not have lower welfare than others who lack his handicap (Dworkin, 2000, p. 60)? Both cases raise some doubts about taking equality of welfare, in either sense, as the underlying standard of fairness.

Another big problem is that people disagree about how important welfare, in either sense, is to the overall value of the lives they lead. Assume we are talking about welfare as happiness or enjoyment. Imagine someone who faces a choice between two possible lives: either life A in which the individual achieves some great intellectual discovery, but in which she is mostly miserable because her efforts still fall short of what she hopes to achieve; or life B in which the individual aims a lot lower, and so is a lot less frustrated and a lot happier, but in which she achieves no great discovery. Which life would you choose: the life of happiness or the life of great achievement? Different people will doubtless make different choices, which shows how we differ on how important welfare, in the sense of happiness, is to a good life. However, if people do disagree about the importance of welfare in a good life, why should they agree to treat welfare as the ultimate good when, as citizens, they are making laws and policies? As Dworkin puts it: 'a political theory of equality based on that [welfarist] conception of the good life is an unattractive theory for a society in which many if not most people reject that conception, and some reject it as alien to their most profound beliefs about the goodness of their own lives' (Dworkin, 2000, p. 44). A similar point applies to the success view of welfare.[2] In contrast, while few people will regard the possession of external and internal resources as the ultimate good in life, everyone can perhaps agree that they are instrumentally important in enabling us to pursue whatever conception of ultimate good we have. Equality of resources has the vital advantage of apparently being more *ecumenical* than equality of welfare as between different philosophies of the good life.

4.2   Resources versus capabilities?

Dworkin's theory has excited many responses and criticisms. One line of criticism, which I will touch on only briefly, focuses on Dworkin's treatment of productive talent. Why should we take the compensation level chosen in the hypothetical insurance market as the appropriate level of compensation for people with poor productive talent? If we really think it is fundamentally unfair for one person to be worse off than another through no fault of their own, then surely the ideally just level of compensation is that which equalizes people's earnings capacities and, incentives considerations aside, anything less is unjust (White, 1999; van der Veen, 2002). Admittedly, in the case of handicaps, the idea of compensation to achieve full equality looks much more problematic: some people might have handicaps that are so bad we could channel society's entire product to them and they would still be at a severe disadvantage compared with others. But even if this means we should adopt the hypothetical insurance approach in thinking about the fair treatment of handicaps, rather than insisting on full equality as the ideally just policy, it is not clear why we should do the same for productive talents. In short, some critics regard Dworkin's treatment of talent inequality as an inadequate reflection of the basic principles he affirms.

Another line of criticism, pressed particularly by G. A. Cohen and Amartya Sen, focuses on Dworkin's insistence that we should concentrate wholly on 'resources' in assessing disadvantage. Cohen argues that while equality of welfare is not adequate as a conception of equality, an adequate conception of equality must give some place to welfare, and that

Dworkin goes too far in trying to close the door on any independent concern for welfare disadvantage. Cohen asks us to imagine an 'unfortunate person' who is able to move his arms very effectively, but who suffers severe pain in his arm muscles afterwards. There is an expensive medicine we could give the man to suppress the pain. In Cohen's view, any egalitarian would surely see that the man has a claim to be given the medicine, in view of its pain-relieving effects. But what motivates this generosity if not a concern for the man's access to *welfare*? To be sure, we could describe the problem the man has as a kind of resource deficiency. We could say he lacks 'the resource of being able to avoid pain [after moving his arms]'. But in saying this we 'would be invoking the idea of equality of opportunity for welfare even if [we] would be using resourcist language to describe it' (G. A. Cohen, 1989, p. 919).

So, Cohen argues, welfare disadvantage does sometimes matter. If this is so, however, then we need to reopen the issue of expensive tastes. Cohen agrees with Dworkin that someone like Louis who cultivates tastes for expensive clarets and plovers' eggs should not be given extra resources to meet their cost. But, says Cohen, the reason is that in the case Dworkin describes, Louis *chooses* to develop these expensive tastes. If people choose to develop expensive tastes, then it is certainly not fair for them to expect others to subsidize them. This is where Dworkin's emphasis on taking responsibility for the consequences of our choices is spot on. However, we can easily imagine a case in which someone inherits an expensive taste. As a result, he or she will likely have lower welfare than others, and this welfare deficit will not be the result of choice but of forces beyond his control. If, like Dworkin, we think that people should be compensated for the bad brute luck of being born with, say, low productive talent, should we not also be concerned to compensate people for the bad brute luck of being born with, or socialized into, expensive tastes? In Cohen's view, the key, if implicit, idea in Dworkin's theory is the powerful idea that egalitarians should be concerned to prevent or correct for disadvantage due to bad brute luck while tolerating that due to choice (including option luck). But Dworkin fails to push the idea to its logical conclusion. Having recognized how financial inheritances and endowments of natural ability can be sources of brute luck disadvantage, he fails to see that a person's tastes can also be a source of brute luck disadvantage (see also Arneson, 1990).

Amartya Sen's analysis starts with a definition of a person's well-being as constituted by the 'functionings' that he or she achieves:

> beings and doings [which] . . . can vary from such elementary things as being adequately nourished, being in good health, avoiding escapable morbidity and premature mortality, etc., to more complex achievements such as being happy, having self-respect, taking part in the life of the community, and so on. (Sen, 1992, p. 39)

A person's *capability* is his or her power to achieve functionings: 'a set of vectors of functionings, reflecting the person's freedom to lead one type of life or another' (Sen, 1992, p. 40). The kind of equality we should want, according to Sen, is in the space of capability, the power or effective freedom to achieve valuable functionings. This capabilities approach is contrasted with approaches that focus, respectively, on welfare and on the resources people have (in the sense of goods or income).

Criticizing welfarism, Sen points out how people can and do adapt their desires and capacity for enjoyment to their circumstances. The poor discipline themselves to be happy and/or fulfilled with little, while the rich forget how to be happy and/or fulfilled unless they have a lot. If our concern is merely to equalize the welfare people have, then, because of 'adaptive preferences', this could entail maintaining huge inequalities of income and wealth (Sen, 1992, pp. 54–5). But in rejecting welfarism we should not accept resourcism. Resourcism is exemplified, in Sen's analysis, by John Rawls's theory which focuses on the distribution of the 'primary goods', notably income and wealth, that citizens have (we will discuss Rawls in chapter 5). Sen's criticism of Rawls – and, by extension, of Dworkin – is that two people can be equal in their income and wealth but still be very unequal in their capability because of differences in health or bodily functioning: 'equality of holdings of primary goods or of resources can go hand in hand with serious inequalities in actual freedoms enjoyed by different persons' (Sen, 1992, p. 81). Resources, in the sense of goods or income, are the *means* to freedom, but they are not *freedom itself*, which, Sen argues, is what we should be concerned with.[3]

Sen's capabilities approach has a lot in common with the approach that Cohen draws out of his even-handed critique of welfarism and Dworkin's resourcism. Both Sen and Cohen subscribe to what one might call a *pluralistic access theory* of equality: when we consider how equal two people are we should focus on their access to a plurality of types of advantage which include, but are not reducible to, welfare.

There remains a good deal of controversy, however, as to whether conceptions of equality like those offered by Cohen and Sen offer a persuasive alternative to Dworkin's (or, indeed, Rawls's) resourcist conception. Recall that for Dworkin a major problem with equality of welfare is that it is not a sufficiently ecumenical conception of equality. It relies on a theory of what makes a life valuable that many reasonable citizens do not endorse. Do the alternatives to equality of welfare proposed by Cohen and Sen do better than equality of welfare in this regard?

On the face of it, Sen's capabilities approach seems acutely vulnerable to this type of criticism. A capability is the power to achieve a specific functioning. But which functionings, out of the multitude that we might focus on, matter? How are we to judge the importance of one type of functioning relative to others? Can we answer these questions without making judgments about what makes for a valuable human life that will be disputed by some reasonable people?

In reply, it can be argued that there are some core, basic capabilities that reasonable people across a very wide range of faiths and philosophies of the good life surely will acknowledge as very important (see also Nussbaum, 1990, 1992, 2000). Capabilities of being well-nourished, adequately clothed and sheltered, for example, are arguably capabilities that have this ecumenical importance. Thus, a focus on select *core capabilities* might not be vulnerable to Dworkin's ecumenicist criticism. Turning to Cohen's arguments, the medicine-for-muscle-pain example suggests that we need to qualify Dworkin's claim that 'welfare' is not a sufficiently ecumenical concern to be the focus of a political theory of equality. Dworkin is right that as a general matter people put a different value on happiness and/or on success in achieving their goals in their overall conceptions of the good life. But they might still agree that *some specific kinds of diswelfare*, such as involuntary, severe physical pain, must be avoided if the life we lead is to be a good one. The capability of avoiding such pain can be seen as one of the core capabilities that is of great and ecumenical importance to people. Thus, we probably can recognize some capability and welfare deficits as a matter of intrinsic concern for a theory of equality without thereby entangling this theory in controversial claims about the nature of the good life. Indeed, Dworkin himself seems to acknowledge this. In response to Cohen's medicine-for-muscle-pain example, Dworkin tells us:

> Almost everyone would agree that a decent life, whatever its other features, is one that is free from serious and enduring physical or mental pain or discomfort, and having a physical or mental infirmity or condition that makes pain or depression or discomfort inescapable without expensive medicine or clothing is therefore an evident and straightforward handicap. (2000, p. 297)

Prudent people in the hypothetical insurance market would probably choose to insure themselves against this handicap, Dworkin argues, and so, according to his theory, it would probably be just for the government to purchase the medicine necessary to suppress the pain suffered by the individual in Cohen's example. Many of the other capability deficits that concern Sen would similarly be treated in Dworkin's scheme as 'handicaps' for which compensation may be due, depending on the choices we think the average person would make in the hypothetical insurance market.

It would seem, then, that at base Dworkin's theory of equality is in fact broadly pluralistic in the way that Cohen and Sen recommend, encompassing a concern for disadvantage that covers not only lack of resources in the ordinary sense of this word but also the lack of some kinds of capabilities, including capabilities for some kinds of welfare. Dworkin obscures this, however, by labelling any disadvantage he accepts as important as a disadvantage in 'resources', stretching the meaning of the term beyond its usual range as, for example, when he writes that a 'pain-producing infirmity' is 'a canonical example of a lack of personal resources' (Dworkin, 2000, p. 297). At the same time, Dworkin's idea of the hypothetical insurance market arguably adds something to the theories of Cohen and Sen. Specifically, one way we might try to identify basic capabilities, of ecumenical importance to people of diverse conceptions of the good, is to ask: Would the vast majority of people in a Dworkin-style insurance market take out a policy against not having this or that particular capability? The hypothetical insurance market perhaps offers a useful thought-experiment that we can use to explore and refine our views about which capabilities, including welfare capabilities, matter enough to be the focus of a political theory of equality.

4.3 Against luck egalitarianism 1: threat to liberty

As we saw in chapter 3, critics object that meritocracy threatens personal liberty. Many of the objections we noted there apply also to luck egalitarianism insofar as it takes on board the equal opportunity demands of meritocracy while also striving to go beyond them. But luck egalitarianism faces at least one further liberty-based objection in view of its strong commitment to the redistribution of labour income from skilled to unskilled workers.

In approaching this objection it is important first to see that redistributive taxation as such does not necessarily just 'reduce' liberty as we usually understand this term. In a market society, the range of actions we are legally permitted to perform – our liberty in the usual sense of the term – depends directly on our income and wealth. If someone tries to take a train from London to Liverpool but has no ticket because she cannot afford the fare, then she may be physically removed from the train long before it reaches its destination. If she goes into a shop to pick up some ingredients for a meal, but cannot pay the shopkeeper for them, then she may be physically stopped from leaving the shop with the ingredients and so she will be prevented from cooking the meal. To do things we need materials (even passive meditation or sleep requires material in the form of a space in which to sit or lie down), and in a society like our own money is the all-purpose ticket we use to get legal title to materials; if we have no money, we can get title to fewer, if any, materials, and so there will be little, if anything, that we are legally entitled to do (G. A. Cohen, 1997; see also Waldron, 1993b; Swift, 2001, pp. 68–71). Thus, if the state intervenes to transfer income and wealth from a rich person to a poor person, it will indeed reduce the range of actions that it is legally permissible for the richer person to perform, but it will also expand the range of actions that it is legally permissible for the poorer person to perform. In this respect, redistribution is not a question of sacrificing liberty for the sake of equality, but of the government acting to create *a more equal liberty*.

Is there, however, something particularly problematic, from the point of view of personal liberty, about taxation of *labour incomes*? Philosophers who belong to the school of thought known as *libertarianism* argue that there is. I will set out the libertarian objection in the remainder of this section and consider how the egalitarian can respond to it.

If you were asked to think of a state of being in which a person is wholly lacking in freedom, what would you think of? Slavery, perhaps? To be a slave is to be the property of another. The other person has full rights of ownership in your body and abilities and, as such, has full legal right to command you to do anything he or she wants. Perhaps the essence of freedom, then, lies in the exact opposite of slavery: in the state of *self-ownership* in which one has full private ownership rights in one's body and abilities.[4] On the face of it, self-ownership certainly looks like an attractive idea: 'my body is my property' is a powerful slogan to throw against those who would like to control how we lead our personal lives.

Now imagine that we have taken the advice of a luck egalitarian philosopher and we have set up a tax-transfer scheme which taxes the labour incomes of talented workers and subsidizes the labour incomes of less talented workers. Imagine that you are a talented worker, able to earn a wage equal to twice your society's average. The government taxes every pound you earn at the rate of 50 per cent and uses the resulting funds to pay subsidies to those who have earnings capacity below the social average (White, 1999). As a result, if you work, then you have no choice but to work, in part, for the benefit of the less talented, though you have not contracted to do so, and, indeed, may not wish to do so. Hence, the libertarian philosopher Robert Nozick comments in his influential book, *Anarchy, State and Utopia*, that: 'Taxation of labor incomes is on a par with forced labor' (Nozick, 1974, p. 169). The talented worker is in effect *part-owned by the less talented workers* and, so the libertarian claims, this denial of full self-ownership makes his or her position relevantly similar to that of a slave.

Egalitarians can respond by pointing to the numerous ways in which the situation of talented workers, under a tax-transfer scheme like that just described, is utterly different to that of a slave. For example, under the tax-transfer scheme just described, it is entirely at the talented worker's discretion as to how long he works. If he chooses to work, then his earnings will get taxed at a certain rate, but he can choose how many hours to work or, indeed, not to work at all. (If, for example, he prefers to stay home while his partner earns the household's income, he may do that.) As to the nature of his work, he has full freedom of occupational choice, and if he doesn't like working for one employer he can always look for a job with another, or try to set up in business on his own. These are all important freedoms that a slave lacks. Thus, it seems absurd to say that egalitarian taxation of labour incomes makes the talented worker into a slave, or puts him or her in a position that is 'on a par with' that of a slave (Christman, 1991; Wolff, 1991; G. A. Cohen, 1995b; chapter 10).

The charge of enslavement is misleading exaggeration. However, I am not sure that this altogether gets the egalitarian off the hook. Silly rhetoric about enslavement aside, the libertarian is stating the truth when he says that under a tax regime akin to that described above, talented workers who choose to work have no choice but to work, in part, for the benefit of others. The tax regime involves what we may call *effort-harnessing*: when a talented person chooses to expend effort for their own benefit in work, these efforts are harnessed through the tax regime so that the less fortunate are, as it were, pulled along with (by) the talented. The talented have no freedom to throw off this 'harness' and work solely for their own benefit. Granted that this does not make the talented workers into slaves, is it nevertheless objectionable to put talented workers into a harness of this kind? Is effort-harnessing in itself an objectionable restriction of personal freedom? Egalitarians think not. They may well be right. But perhaps this is a question that warrants more consideration.[5]

4.4 Against luck egalitarianism 2: social and political inequality

Imagine a society that has enacted luck egalitarianism in full with no qualification. What would such a society look like? Well, for one thing, it could well have some people who are in dire need. Take the case of Arnold, a young man who, in his eagerness to get to a business meeting, turned a corner in his car at high speed and crashed. As a result, Arnold is disabled and finds it hard to earn a living. But the government refuses to give him much assistance, arguing that the disadvantage he suffers largely reflects his own bad option luck. On the other hand, consider the case of Beryl. Beryl is quite a lazy and unenterprising individual, but one day she buys a lucky lottery ticket on her way home from the pub and wins millions of pounds. The government does not tax her wealth as it results from her good option luck. A luck egalitarian utopia (or dystopia?) is a society in which there are lottery millionaires like Beryl and destitute disabled people like Arnold. People like Arnold might sit at the gates of the mansions of people like Beryl and ask for assistance. Perhaps the Beryls will assist the Arnolds. Or perhaps not.

In view of these and other apparent implications, some philosophers have argued that luck egalitarianism is fundamentally misguided. The alleged problem is not so much that it is too egalitarian, but that it is not egalitarian *in the right way*. As the examples of Arnold and Beryl show, it would permit the emergence of significant economic inequalities which could, in turn, produce significant inequalities in power and in social status. Luck egalitarianism stands condemned, in short, because it is apparently at odds with the values of political and social equality. This line of argument is advanced very forcefully by Elizabeth Anderson (Anderson, 1999; see also Scheffler, 2003). Anderson first criticizes the attitude of luck egalitarians to those, like Arnold, who suffer disadvantage due to lifestyle choice and bad option luck. As noted, a luck egalitarian will argue that society has a very limited obligation to assist a disabled person like Arnold, for their disability is not the result of bad brute luck but of bad option luck. But according to Anderson, justice cannot require us, or even permit us, to abandon someone to disability in this way. Doing so will leave the person concerned far too vulnerable to oppression by others and to exploitation and abuse (see also Goodin, 1986). A second flaw with luck egalitarianism, Anderson argues, is that it treats the 'untalented' and 'handicapped' in a demeaning way. It seeks to compensate them for their poor internal resources. But the compensatory attitude can all too easily express a message of condescending pity. Anderson imagines a 'State Equality Board' sending letters out to people with poor internal resources, explaining why they are being sent compensation. One imagined letter reads:

> To the ugly and socially awkward: How sad that you are so repulsive to people around you that no one wants to be your friend or lifetime companion. We won't make it up to you by being your friend or marriage partner – we have our own freedom of association to exercise – but you can console yourself in your miserable loneliness by consuming these material goods, that we, the beautiful and charming ones, will provide. (Anderson, 1999, p. 305)

Anderson's point here is reminiscent of Michael Young's critique of meritocracy which we discussed in chapter 3. Young argues that meritocracy will undermine status equality by encouraging the people who lose in meritocratic competition to feel inferior, while those who succeed regard themselves as essentially superior. Anderson is saying that the luck egalitarian emphasis on compensation for poor internal resources might similarly generate attitudes of inferiority and superiority and so undermine status equality.

Anderson's alternative to luck egalitarianism treats the issue of economic equality as something that is to be wholly determined by our concerns for social and political equality. She argues that, properly understood, egalitarianism has two central aims. One is to *abolish oppression*: 'forms of social relationship by which some people dominate, exploit, marginalize, demean, and inflict violence upon others' (Anderson, 1999, p. 313). The second is to create a *democratic community*, a society in which there is 'collective self-determination by means of open discussion among equals, according to rules which can be accepted by all' (Anderson, 1999, p. 313). To achieve these aims, government must regulate the distribution of income and wealth, ensuring that people at all times have ready access to the resources necessary to avoid oppressive social relationships and to participate fully in democratic government. But equality of income and wealth is not the goal in itself. We need only as much equality in income and wealth as is necessary to prevent oppression and ensure that all can participate fully in democratic politics. Moreover, these objectives will require not only redistribution of income and wealth, but action to change social attitudes towards marginalized groups such as the disabled and gays and lesbians. In Nancy Fraser's terms, there is as much need for a politics of 'recognition', in which respect for historically disadvantaged groups is publicly affirmed, as a politics of 'redistribution' (Fraser, 1995; see also Satz, 1996; Wolff, 1998).

For want of a better term, let us call Anderson's type of approach to economic equality the *status-power approach*: we should treat economic inequality as an issue wholly or primarily in terms of its implications for inequality in status and/or power (both power within personal relationships and in the political process). Elements of the status-power approach to economic equality in fact have a long history within political thought. For instance, the argument that economic inequality must be moderated so as to secure equality in the political sphere is central to the civic republican tradition. In *The Social Contract* Rousseau makes the republican argument that economic inequality will generate instability that threatens political equality:

If you wish to give the state cohesion, bring the limits of wealth and poverty as close together as possible: do not allow either extreme opulence or destitution. The two are inseparable by nature, and both are equally damaging to the common good; one produces the instruments of tyranny, and the other produces the tyrants. It is always between them that public liberty is traded, one buying and the other selling. (Rousseau, 1994 [1762], p. 87, note 1)

The argument that economic inequality is bad because it threatens status equality, and should be reduced for this reason, is one we find in some British socialist thinkers. R. H. Tawney, for example, supported greater economic equality as necessary to status equality and to the sense of 'fellowship' that this would make possible (Tawney, 1964 [1931]).

What might the luck egalitarian say in reply to Anderson and other supporters of the status-power approach to economic inequality?

First, she might question whether Anderson has given a wholly correct account of what luck egalitarians are committed to. It is not clear, for example, that luck egalitarians such as Dworkin are necessarily committed only to responding to poor internal resources with offers of monetary compensation. There is nothing inherent in luck egalitarianism in general, or in Dworkin's theory in particular, which says that those with 'handicaps' must receive monetary compensation rather than benefitting from measures to combat prejudice or to integrate them better into society. The 'insurance policies' that people buy in Dworkin's hypothetical insurance market can be readily understood to include measures of this integrative, rather than just those of a narrowly compensatory, kind. Moreover, while Anderson is surely right to point to the desirability of an integrative response to those with disabilities, there is still the difficult question of just how much society should spend on such a response. Given that resources are scarce, we cannot necessarily spend up to the point where the marginal benefit in terms of social integration is zero. A thought-experiment like Dworkin's hypothetical insurance market might help us get a handle on the difficult question of how much it is fair for society to spend on policies of integration.

Second, the luck egalitarian can argue that some of Anderson's objectives are ill-served by altogether ignoring the distinctions that luck egalitarians draw. For example, some would argue that status equality will be undermined by arrangements under which one group of hard-working citizens is required continually to subsidize others who can work but who choose not to (Kaus, 1992; Mead, 1992). Can one regard able-bodied people who choose to live off your labours all the time as equals, particularly as their choice to do so seems to express disrespect towards you? Anderson herself accepts that basic income entitlements can be made conditional on work (Anderson, 1999, p. 318), and in this respect her proposed alternative to luck egalitarianism recommends a social policy that is not all that different to that of (some) luck egalitarians.[6]

Third, and most fundamentally, is Anderson right to think that inequality in the distribution of income and wealth matters, morally speaking, only insofar as it relates to inequalities in status and power? Granted that the implications of economic inequality for status and power inequality do matter morally, why should one think that these specific implications exhaust the moral significance of economic inequality? Inequality in income and wealth affects our life-chances in so many myriad ways we should surely regard it as an issue of justice *in its own right*, and not only insofar as it impacts on status and power inequality. If so, then we cannot regard the status-power approach as sufficient, but must to look to other approaches, such as luck egalitarianism, to inform our understanding of what makes for a fully fair distribution of income and wealth.

However, these points only suggest that we ought not wholly to reject luck egalitarianism in favour of the status-power approach. They do not necessarily imply that we should rest content with luck egalitarianism to the exclusion of the status-power approach. The rather grim world of Arnold and Beryl depicted at the start of this section suggests that there is indeed something defective in luck egalitarianism conceived as the sole guide to creating a 'society of equals' (Scheffler, 2003). We seem to need the insights of the status-power approach to enrich and qualify luck egalitarianism, even if it should not simply replace it. But this is much more easily said than done. Bringing the two perspectives together is clearly going to be a challenging task as their standard prescriptions sometimes conflict. Perhaps there is a theory to be discovered that will balance and integrate the insights of the two perspectives. Or it may be that we have to learn to live with both perspectives, to accept the points of tension between them, and to grapple even-handedly with the hard choices that these tensions present. As Bernard Williams helpfully says:

> When one is faced with the spectacle of various elements of the idea of equality pulling in these different directions, there is a strong temptation, if one does not abandon the idea altogether, to abandon some of its elements. . . . To succumb [to this temptation] would, I think, be a mistake. . . . we should not throw one set of claims out of the window. . . . It is an uncomfortable situation, but the discomfort is just that of genuine political thought. It is not greater with equality than it is with liberty, or any other noble and substantial political ideal. (Williams, 1973, pp. 248–9)

5
Equality and Incentives

There are in truth other motives to work than those of direct and proportionate pecuniary reward. There is the hope of advancement, of social esteem, there is the pure love of work, and the desire to serve society.
Leonard Hobhouse, *The Labour Movement*, 1912

Many people who think economic equality is desirable in principle might reject it in practice because of what they perceive to be its damaging effects on economic incentives, in particular incentives to work. In this chapter we will explore how proponents of economic equality have responded to this long-standing criticism.

Assuming that allowing inequality does have an incentive effect which raises output, how much inequality ought we to permit? Section 5.1 sketches three preliminary answers to this question. One of these is John Rawls's proposal that we should permit inequality to the point where it maximizes the position of the class that is worst off under inequality. Section 5.2 explores in more detail the arguments for and against this proposal. Section 5.3 then examines an important objection to Rawls's approach: that in presenting incentive-based inequality that raises the position of the worst off as just, Rawls concedes too much to the selfishness of talented workers. In a just society, the critic argues, talented workers would not demand special incentive payments as the price of deploying their scarce talents. Section 5.4 follows on from this by considering how (if at all) an economy might function efficiently without the use of special monetary incentives. Is such an economy conceivable and defensible as a moral ideal? Section 5.5 wraps up with a provisional summary of what we have learned about the economic dimension of equality in chapters 3 through 5.

5.1   Incentives and inequality: three views

What is the incentives argument for economic inequality? The basic intuition is well put by the British politician Douglas Jay:

> many of those whose skill, character, knowledge or experience [are] above the lowest would not use their ability fully if they earned no more than those who contributed less. Therefore, the whole output of goods and services would be less, and society as a whole would be poorer. (Jay, 1962, p. 8)

An insistence on strict equality in rewards for work would reduce the motivation of more talented workers, depressing output. So some inequality should be permitted as a way of encouraging the talented to work hard. But just how much inequality should we allow in order to raise output?

One answer is: we should allow inequality to the level required to maximize total output. This is one way of understanding what Jay says in the passage above.[1] However, if we look at the work of an earlier thinker, Leonard Hobhouse, we find a different view of the standard we should use to assess inequality of reward. In his book, *The Labour Movement*, Hobhouse argues that every worker should receive the income necessary to ensure the permanent health of himself, his whole family, and his ability to be an effective citizen of a democratic society.[2] All workers should at least get this, either directly or via transfers from the state. Like Jay, Hobhouse thinks that we will have to pay some workers more than this in order to bring forth their best efforts:

We have agreed that every one who is employed at all should receive the minimim wage. Could we, then, expect for the same wage to get men to face the most arduous and unpleasant forms of work, to acquire and apply the highest skill, to put forth the utmost of their efforts, to give us the best of their brain power? We might expect these results in Utopia, but not, I fear, in the world as we know it. . . . [Thus if] we found that we could not get the ability that we required at a given rate, we should have to raise the rate. (Hobhouse, 1912, pp. 34–5)

But Hobhouse explicitly sees the right of all workers to a decent minimum wage as setting a limit to how much inequality of reward is acceptable: 'If any particular form of ability required so much of us that to pay for it we should have to deplete the fund available for ordinary labour, we should have to put it down as too expensive' (Hobhouse, 1912, p. 35). So Hobhouse will only permit us to raise output through inequality of rewards subject to the constraint that every worker receives at least a high minimum income. We may not raise total output at the price of depriving any worker of a decent minimum.

There is a third position that we need to consider. This is set out in John Rawls's book, *A Theory of Justice* (1999a [1971]). In this book, Rawls sets out and tries to defend a conception of justice to govern the design of society's major institutions. The conception he defends includes the following influential idea: 'social and economic inequalities are to be arranged so that they are . . . to the greatest benefit of the least advantaged' (Rawls, 1999a, p. 72). This expresses what Rawls calls the *difference principle*. Applied to our present discussion, and for the moment simplifying a little, the difference principle implies something like this: it is acceptable (it is just) to move from equality to inequality of reward only so long as this improves how much we are able to pay to the class of lowest-paid workers. So inequality of reward may be increased (moving away from equality) up to the point where any further inequality would cause a fall in the pay and living standards of the class of workers who receive the lowest pay. Whereas Hobhouse wants to ensure that all workers get at least a decent minimum, Rawls says that in arranging inequality of reward we should aim to make the worst-off workers as well off as possible – which may well entail their having more than merely a decent minimum.

Here, then, we have three distinct views as to how much inequality of reward we should allow on incentives grounds: (1) we should allow whatever level of inequality serves to maximize total output; (2) we should allow inequality that raises total output but subject to the constraint that every worker is guaranteed a decent minimum (Hobhouse); and (3) we should allow that level of inequality that makes the group of worst-off workers as well off as possible (Rawls). On reasonable assumptions, the first position is likely to prescribe more inequality than Hobhouse's, which in turn will prescribe more inequality than Rawls's. This can be illustrated using figure 5.1.

The horizontal axis in figure 5.1 measures the level of inequality of reward (increasing as we move away from the origin). The vertical axis shows the effect of different levels of inequality on the average income of the whole population (line AVG) and on the income of the class of lowest-paid workers (line LPD). Line MIN represents the level of income a worker typically needs to have a decent life. In the society

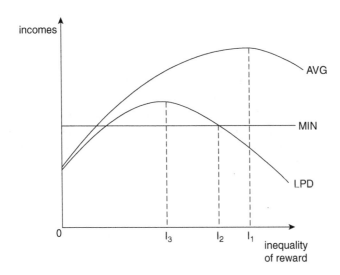

Figure 5.1   How much inequality of reward?

represented in figure 5.1, how much inequality of reward would be selected by each of our three standards? If we follow the first view then we will select inequality at point I_1. This is the point at which average income is highest and for a given population this will also be the point at which total output is highest. But note how, in this society, the income of the class of lowest-paid workers is actually lower than the decent minimum at the point at which average income is maximized. Hobhouse would not allow us to raise inequality to I_1 because some workers are not getting a decent minimum with this level of inequality. Were we to follow Hobhouse's standard we would have to select the level of inequality at point I_2. This is the point at which average income and total output is at its highest while workers in the lowest-paid class still get a decent income. However, in this society, workers in the lowest-paid class are still not as well off as they could be. Were we to select inequality of reward at point I_3, then the lowest-paid group of workers would be better off than they would be at any other level of inequality. This is the level of inequality of reward that Rawls prescribes. In moving from the first standard to Hobhouse's to Rawls's we move progressively to lower levels of inequality – though the level of inequality that satisfies Rawls's standard could still be quite high.

Thus far I have simply laid out the three positions. Of the three, the first position seems obviously wrong. It surely cannot be fair to allow inequality to maximize total output if the effect is also to push some workers below a decent minimum (I suspect that Jay would have accepted this point if he had been pressed to clarify his view). However, of the two remaining positions, it is not so obvious which we should adopt. To explore this issue further, let us take a closer look at Rawls's difference principle and the arguments he makes for it.

5.2   Defending the difference principle

Rawls considers himself to be addressing the citizen of a deliberative democracy (see chapter 2; J. Cohen, 2003). He proposes that the citizen try to identify principles of justice, to guide legislation, through the use of a social contract thought-experiment. Specifically, the citizen is to imagine a group of people who are ignorant of their actual or likely position in society; they don't know what skills they have, what social class they are born into, or even what religion they have. The citizen must then ask herself: What principles would people behind this 'veil of ignorance' agree to?

Rawls argues that the people in this 'original position' would select a conception of justice ('justice as fairness') consisting of the following two principles:

> First: each person is to have an equal right to the most extensive basic liberty compatible with a similar liberty for others.
>
> Second: social and economic inequalities are to be arranged so that they are both (a) to the greatest benefit of the least advantaged and (b) attached to offices and positions open to all under conditions of fair equality of opportunity. (Rawls, 1999a, p. 71)

The second principle, which is the one we shall focus on here, has two components. One component, part (b) in the above definition, is the requirement of 'fair equality of opportunity'. This is the requirement that:

> those with similar abilities and skills should have similar life chances . . . those who are at the same level of talent and ability, and have the same willingness to use them, should have the same prospects of success regardless of their initial place in the social system. (Rawls, 1999a, p. 73)

This is the type of equality of opportunity associated with strong meritocracy (chapter 3). However, Rawls does not think that strong meritocracy is sufficient for justice (though it is necessary). The other component of his second principle of justice, part (a) in the above definition, is the difference principle. This demands that 'social and economic inequalities' be arranged to maximize the prospects of the worst off group. In other words, starting from a position of strict equality, we may permit inequality provided that by doing so we somehow make those left worst off under the inequality better off than they would be under strict equality. We may, indeed should, increase inequality to the point at which the position of the worst off is as good as it would be at any other level of inequality.[3] Strictly speaking, the difference principle regulates inequality in an index of goods which include income and wealth, but also 'powers and prerogatives of offices and positions of responsibility' and the 'the social bases of self-respect' (see Pogge, 1989, pp. 162–4; and Van Parijs, 2003, for helpful discussions).[4] In effect, this is Rawls's way of saying that in thinking about fairness in economic arrangements we need to factor in concerns that this book has put under the heading of social equality.[5] For instance, although the low paid might get relatively high incomes under an economic system that generates great income inequality, this income inequality might also give rise to status inequality which damages their self-respect. Overall, taking into account the impact on self-respect, the low paid may be better off under a system which gives them lower incomes but which also has greater income equality and, thereby, status equality (Pogge, 1989, p. 163). It is sometimes convenient to simplify discussion of the difference principle, as I shall here, by talking as if it is just a guide to the distribution of income and wealth, but it should be kept in mind when we do so that this is indeed a simplification.

When Rawls started work on his theory of social justice, political thought was still strongly influenced by a philosophy from the nineteenth century, Utilitarianism, which says that we should design social institutions so as to maximize total happiness (Bentham, 1996 [1789]; Mill, 1993a [1861]). It was important for Rawls to make the case that 'justice as fairness' gives a better account of justice than Utilitarianism. Consequently, he imagines that the parties in the original position face a choice between the difference principle and a version of Utilitarianism, the principle of average welfare (the principle which says we should arrange social institutions so as to maximize the average welfare of people in society).[6] He argues that the parties have good reason to choose the difference principle over the average welfare principle.

On the face of it, it is by no means clear that this is the obvious choice. To be sure, the difference principle is in a sense the safest choice. If, when the veil of ignorance lifts, you find yourself in society's worst-off group, then under the difference principle you will be better off (or at least as well off) than you would be under any other principle. But what if, when the veil lifts, you discover that in fact you are at the top end of society? In this case, you will almost certainly be worse off under the difference principle than you would be under the average welfare principle. The choice the parties in the original position face is between one option that will protect them well if they turn out to be poor, but not serve them well if they turn out to be rich (the difference principle), and another option that will likely be much better for them if they turn out to be rich, but potentially disastrous for them if they turn out to be poor (the average welfare principle). A question that many critics of Rawls have pressed is: Why don't the people in the original position take a gamble on the second option? Why should they play it safe?

Perhaps Rawls's best answer to why people in the original position should not take such a gamble appeals to an idea he calls 'strains of commitment' (Rawls, 1999a, pp. 153–4). The thought is that in agreeing principles of justice, the people in the original position must accept that they are making a decision that is final. They must honestly be able to say to themselves and to each other that they can live with the principles chosen in the future whatever the consequences turn out to be. They must honestly be able to say that they can bear the strains of commitment. Now under the principle of average welfare, the people in society's worst-off group could be very badly off indeed. It is possible, for example, that average welfare might be maximized by enslaving a small fraction of the population: while this would be very bad for the welfare of the enslaved, it is always possible that this would be outweighed on the average by welfare gains to everyone else from having slaves to call on. But if the lot of the worst off under the average welfare principle is potentially so bad, people in the original position cannot honestly say that they could bear the strains of living under this principle regardless of the class in society they turn out to be in. In contrast, the difference principle guarantees the worst off a good life (or at least as good a life as they could get under any principle) and so should not place unbearable strains on anyone. Hence, people in the original position should commit to it rather than the principle of average welfare.[7]

While this is quite a persuasive argument, one might wonder if Rawls has not made life a bit easy for himself by restricting the choice in the original position to one between the difference principle and the principle of average welfare. One can readily imagine a third option, a principle of 'floor-constrained' average welfare which says: arrange social institutions so as to maximize average welfare subject to the constraint that everybody has ready access to a decent minimum of income. This is reasonably close, in fact, to Hobhouse-like principles of maximizing total output or average income subject to the constraint that every working family receive a decent minimum of income. Would intermediate principles of this kind – 'floor-constrained maximization principles', to use an ugly phrase – seem more attractive to parties in the original position than either the difference principle or the average welfare principle? On the one hand, such principles ensure that if, when the veil lifts, you find yourself in society's worst-off group, then you won't be too badly off: you'll have ready access to a decent minimum. On the other hand, if you find yourself at the top of society, the likelihood is that you will be better off than in a society regulated by the difference principle. Some kind of floor-constrained maximization principle looks like a happy medium between the two alternatives that Rawls offers.[8] Appeal to strains of commitment isn't so obviously decisive here. Floor-constrained maximization principles guarantee everyone ready access to a decent minimum, so presumably the strains of commitment for the worst off are bearable (Waldron, 1993c).

On further inspection, however, floor-constrained maximization principles look less attractive. One problem has to do with the ambiguity and political contestability of what the floor should consist in (Rawls, 2001, pp. 127–8). As Ronald Dworkin points out:

> once it is conceded that comfortable members of society do not owe their uncomfortable fellow citizens equality, but only some decent minimum standard of living, then too much is allowed to turn on the essentially subjective question of how minimum a standard is decent, and contemporary history

suggests that the comfortable are unlikely to give a generous answer to that question. (Dworkin, 2000, p. 3)

What is a decent minimum? A bare subsistence? More than a bare subsistence? How much more? How much income and wealth do people need to have a super-subsistence minimum? Is there a risk that richer groups in society will push for and effect stingy answers to these difficult questions? If so, then this gives the parties in the original position a reason to be wary of floor-constrained maximization principles. Having agreed to such a principle, and finding themselves in the worst-off group, they might discover that the floor is pitched so low that the strains of commitment do become quite severe.

Rawls also presents a more direct or 'intuitive' argument for the difference principle (Kymlicka, 2000, pp. 57–60). As we noted in chapter 3, Rawls argues that economic inequalities attributable to good fortune in the genetic lottery are just as arbitrary, morally speaking, as those due to unequal fortune in terms of the class and family that one is born into. Naturally gifted workers are not intrinsically deserving of higher income or wealth by virtue of their greater talents, and so we must start from the *presumption* that talented and untalented workers should receive equal incomes and wealth. Morally speaking, strict equality is the appropriate baseline and we have to ask what could possibly justify a departure from it. Well, what if departing from strict equality would lift all boats, including those of the worst off? Surely this would justify inequality. Going back to the levelling-down objection discussed in chapter 1, would we really want to insist on sticking to strict equality when this has the effect of making everyone, including the people who will be worst off under inequality, worse off? One might try to recast the argument in terms of a social contract agreed between groups who know their respective talents (an approach critically explored in Barry, 1989, pp. 229–34). The talented say to the untalented: 'Look, I know we don't deserve the higher incomes we can obtain under inequality, but you should agree to them because it's also in your interest: you, too, will be better off.' Insofar as this is the case, then it would seem rational for the untalented to consent to inequality. And if *they* agree to it, how can it be wrong? (Important note: we have assumed that inequality lifts all boats, including that of the worst off. This neglects the possibility that, if there are more than two groups, increasing inequality beyond a certain point could improve the position of the top and worst-off groups, while worsening that of intermediate groups. We shall return to this possibility below.)

The difference principle remains controversial. One line of criticism focuses on Rawls's treatment of effort. In a market economy, two workers might have different levels of earnings because one works harder than the other, or because one has more ability, or for both reasons. In *A Theory of Justice*, Rawls suggests that we should not try to differentiate income shares between people according to judgments about how much productive effort they have made. Effort, he argues, is strongly influenced by other factors, such as class background and natural ability (Rawls, 1999a, pp. 64, 89); it is, at any rate, too difficult to disentangle the role of effort from these other influences to make judgments of individual desert based on effort (p. 274). However, this leaves Rawls open to the objection that the difference principle apparently requires hard-working citizens to subsidize the lazy (Musgrave, 1974). What if the people in the lowest income group in society are there because they have chosen to opt out of employment and spend their life surfing? Is it really fair to expect harder-working citizens to foot the bill for such lifestyles? Some philosophers, such as Samuel Scheffler, have argued that Rawls's ideas go too far in contradicting 'common-sense' notions of desert in this case (Scheffler, 1992; see also Kymlicka, 2000, pp. 72–5).

In fact, Rawls's position on this matter is more complex than this criticism suggests. In later work, Rawls emphasizes that people who choose leisure over work should not be seen as entitled to the minimum income share guaranteed by the difference principle (Rawls, 2001, p. 179). The leisure itself, he argues, should be seen as equivalent in value to the income and wealth enjoyed by the lowest income group in employment. If you choose the leisure, you forego the right to the income. This 'expresses the idea that all citizens are to do their part in society's cooperative work' (Rawls, 2001, p. 179). What these later comments suggest is that we are to understand the question of justice in the distribution of income and wealth as a question posed with reference to individuals who are all *citizen-workers*. The question, in effect, is: To what extent can we justify inequality in shares of the social product between citizens who all participate in the creation of this product? But you have to be making (or be willing to make) some productive effort to be included in the share-out. Understood in this way, the gap that Scheffler perceives between Rawls's theory and 'common-sense' notions of desert is much less marked.

A second criticism of the difference principle focuses on the interests of intermediate groups in society. Imagine a society in which there are three social groups: A, very talented; B, moderately talented; and C, untalented. Imagine that we have to choose between two possible economic systems, system X and system Y, which offer the three social groups rewards as set out in table 5.1.

Applying the difference principle we would conclude that system Y is preferable to X because it gives the worst-off group, C, an income of 11 rather than 10. But what about the interests of group B? In choosing Y over X we impose a large sacrifice on its members, a cut of over 50 per cent in its income. Is this substantial loss to members of group B justified by the apparently rather marginal gain to members of group C? Of course, it's hard to evaluate such a case unless we know more about the reality behind these numbers. If, for example, the difference between 10 and 11 is in reality the difference between slow starvation and subsistence, then there is obviously good reason to prefer Y over X despite the big sacrifice it imposes on members of group B. But if the

Table 5.1 The difference principle when 'chain connection' fails

	System X	System Y
Group A	50	45
Group B	30	14
Group C	10	11
Average*	30	23.3

* The averages are calculated on the assumption that there are equal numbers of people in each group.

gain to the worst-off group is in reality rather slight, and the costs to intermediate groups are substantial, then it is not intuitively obvious that we should give *absolute* priority to the interests of the worst-off group, as the difference principle demands (Dworkin, 2000, pp. 330–1). Rawls assumes that the position of intermediate groups tends to improve with that of the worst-off group, starting to worsen only when that of the worst-off group starts to worsen. This is the principle of 'chain connection' (Rawls, 1999a, pp. 69–72). It may be that this assumption holds in many societies most of the time. But there is always the possibility that it doesn't hold, and then this criticism might kick in.

In view of this criticism, some thinkers who are sympathetic to Rawls argue that we should consider a principle of giving 'loose' priority to the worst-off group rather than the strict priority that the difference principle demands: as a rule of thumb we should allow inequality to the point where it maximizes the position of the worst-off group, but we allow for some departure from this principle if and when its strict application would cause very large losses to intermediate groups for genuinely very small gains to the worst off (see Nagel, 1991, p. 73; Van Parijs, 1995, p. 42, note 52). Nevertheless, these thinkers would argue that we should stick fairly closely to the difference principle. Even when intermediate groups give up a lot they will still be better off than society's worst-off group. Thomas Nagel argues that we should imagine ourselves in the position of each group and consider how urgent its claims seem compared to those of other groups. Precisely because the worst-off group is worst off, its claims will ordinarily have more urgency than those of others and, accordingly, should usually be given priority (Nagel, 1979).

5.3   The question of work ethos

Let's say that we accept the difference principle, at least a 'loose' variant of it. How much inequality of reward are we likely to have to admit in practice under this principle? This is an empirical question, but one factor that will influence

how far inequality is needed on incentives grounds is the
values of workers themselves and how these affect their attitude to work. For example, the more that workers with scarce
talents can be motivated to apply them from a sense of social
service, or out of intrinsic pleasure in doing a valuable job
well, the less society will have to resort to monetary incentives to call forth their productive efforts, and so the more
equality in reward can be had for a given level of output. Recognizing this, Hobhouse argued that: 'We want a new spirit
in economics. . . . We want each man [sic] to feel that his daily
work is a service to his kind' (Hobhouse, 1912, p. 75; see
also Tawney, 1948 [1921]). At the limit people of all skills
would work to their best from a sense of civic duty and be
happy to receive the same income in return, or else an income
suited to the respective needs of their households. Such a
society would satisfy the communist slogan 'From each
according to his ability, to each according to his needs!'
(Marx, in McLellan (ed.), 1977 [1875], p. 569). Hobhouse
did not expect that society would ever fully reach this ideal.
But, in common with many contemporary and later
Marxists,[9] he certainly thought that society could and should
get closer to it by encouraging a more cooperative work
ethos. Referring back to figure 5.1, a shift to a progressively
more public-spirited work ethos will shift curves AVG and
LPD gradually to the left. As these curves shift leftwards,
the level of inequality required by the difference principle
will fall.

However, while the issue of work ethos is raised in
Hobhouse's work, and by many Marxist writers, it is not discussed by Rawls. This has led some critics, notably G. A.
Cohen, to argue that Rawls's theory concedes too much to
the potential selfishness of talented workers (G. A. Cohen,
1995a [1992], 2000, chapters 8–9). Cohen's critique of
Rawls, to be discussed in the remainder of this section, raises
a basic question that our discussion has so far ignored: To
what extent do talented workers act unjustly when they
demand special incentive payments as the price of deploying
their special skills and talents? Should they, as a matter of
justice, be willing to deploy these skills for no more than an
average social wage, thereby making special incentive payments unnecessary?

Imagine, then, a society with a class of talented workers and a class of untalented workers. We could tax the talented, and subsidize the untalented, so as to equalize the reward they receive (call this the high-tax policy). Or we could put a much lower tax on the talented, subsidize the untalented less, and accept inequality (call this the low-tax policy). A Rawlsian incentives argument for the low-tax policy says that under lower taxes the talented will choose to produce more than they would choose to produce under the high-tax policy, and that some of this extra output can then be harvested for the benefit of the untalented so that they, too, are better off than they would be under the high-tax policy. Clearly a key plank in the argument is the contention that the *talented workers will behave differently under the low-tax policy* (they will work harder). However, Cohen argues that we must then ask: Is the difference in behaviour under the low-tax policy itself justifiable? After all, if the talented workers made the choice to work just as hard under the high-tax policy, then society would still get the full output of their talents, but because the fruits would be more equally shared the untalented workers would be better off than they are under the low-tax policy. Thus, if talented workers make a choice to work less hard under the high-tax policy, then they are choosing to behave in a way that worsens the living standards of less fortunate workers. Could any talented worker look an untalented worker in the eye and justify this choice?[10] In particular, if the talented worker is the citizen of a Rawlsian society, and so claims to believe in the principle that inequality is justifiable only if it is necessary to raise the position of the worst off, how can he or she justify making choices that will make the less fortunate workers poorer than they need be?

In a just society, Cohen argues, egalitarian values, such as a Rawlsian concern for the position of the least advantaged, will govern not only the formal structures of economic cooperation – the laws about taxation and the like – but also the *ethos* that people act from within these structures (G. A. Cohen, 2000, pp. 117–33). Of course, in the absence of such an ethos, then it is sensible for a government to allow inequalities in reward that help to motivate the talented and thereby raise output for the benefit of the worst off. But these inequalities will not be truly just precisely because they are only made necessary, in an immediate sense, by the lack of an appropriate ethos on the part of society's talented workers. Clearly, the fundamental question here is whether talented workers necessarily do something objectionable when they demand special incentive payments for deploying their talents in the most productive ways. Do they?

Consider first the case of Clare, a talented worker who faces a choice between working in two jobs (for a similar example, see Williams, 1998; Daniels, 2003, p. 266). First, she can work as an artist, earning $50,000 a year for her work, which happens to be her society's average wage. Alternatively, she can work as a self-employed computer programmer, generating computer games for export which earn her, before any tax, $200,000 a year. Clare's personal values are such that, for a given amount of earnings, she would much prefer to work as an artist than as a computer programmer. She believes that art brings her closer to God than writing computer games would. She is willing to work as a computer programmer only if she can earn at least $100,000 per year (with this amount of money she believes she can pursue her spiritual life in other ways than by art, for example, by taking expensive meditation courses). Thus, if the tax rate on her earnings in her highest-paying job is more than 50 per cent, she will choose to do art rather than computer programming, and society will lose $150,000 worth of output, a large portion of which would have been available for distribution to members of the worst-off group. Now, recalling Cohen's point, Clare *could* choose to work at computer programming even if the tax rate were, say, 60 per cent. By refusing to do so, she is choosing to act in a way that makes the worst-off group in society worse off than they need be. But, in view of the reasons for her refusal, can we really say that she is acting unjustly? It is not a matter of her acting strategically, sitting on her talents, effectively going on strike to extort as much income as possible in return for her services. She is simply someone with particular religious beliefs, who consequently has a strong preference for one line of work over another, and who is accordingly unwilling to work in the way that is most beneficial to society unless she receives an above-average wage that will enable her to realize her beliefs in another manner. If we insisted that she take her most productive job for an average social wage regardless of her beliefs, then arguably this would be unjust to her. Consider now the case of Dean. Dean has an exceptional talent: he is the only person in his society who can construct truly challenging Su Doku puzzles for the many people who love solving them. He refuses to deploy this rare talent, however, unless he is paid a sum well in excess of the average social wage. He insists on this because he values the resulting inequality between himself and others *for its own sake*. He wants to be able to swank about town, showing off his expensive clothes. He wants to rub other people's noses in the fact that he has more income than they do. His other job option is a job he would not find unpleasant, though, as it does not pay as much, it would not give him the chance to swank. In this kind of case, there does seem something objectionable about the demand for the special incentive payment, given Dean's grubby motivation for demanding it.

The defensibility of incentive demands thus seems to depend on the reason or motivation for them (Estlund, 1998; Williams, 1998; J. Cohen, 2001; Pogge, 2000; Daniels, 2003, pp. 263–270).[11] Cohen himself accepts that there is a sphere of reasonable self-interest in work decisions (G. A. Cohen, 1995a [1992], pp. 370–1), and we might regard Clare's case as one of reasonable self-interest. But Dean's case is probably not one of reasonable self-interest, given the ugly character of his reason for wanting to be paid above the average social wage. So, some incentives payments are probably consistent with justice, all things considered; others not.

This finding moderates, but does not altogether refute, Cohen's critique of incentives-based inequality. Before we can say that an incentives-based inequality is just we need to look at the kind of reasons and motivations that talented workers have for refusing to work as productively as they can for an average social wage. Related to this, we can agree with Cohen that in a just society citizens' work decisions will be governed by an ethos that tempers demands for special incentives payments – an ethos that, for example, discourages talented workers from demanding incentive payments because, like Dean in our example above, they value inequality for its own sake. The interesting issues for future research lie in achieving a fuller sense of reasonable and unreasonable self-interest in work motivation and in assessing exactly how society can and may nurture a work ethos that effectively discourages incentives claims based on unreasonable self-interest.[12]

5.4 Moral incentives in a market economy

Thinkers like Hobhouse and Cohen argue that we should seek to foster a more public-spirited work ethos. But some critics might challenge their vision of a public-spirited economy as unworkable. A tolerably efficient economy must be based on the market (Miller, 1989a; Roemer, 1994, pp. 37–45). But, so the argument runs, markets work because people are motivated by material self-interest. Take away the self-interest, and you take away the motives that direct the 'invisible hand' to efficient outcomes.

A forceful reply to this objection is set out by Joseph Carens in his book, *Equality, Moral Incentives, and the Market* (Carens, 1981). Carens begins his analysis by asking us to imagine a competitive capitalist economy in which work and production decisions are motivated by individuals' self-interested desires for personal income and consumption. He then asks us to imagine that this economy is transformed in the following three ways:

(1) all people believe that they have a social duty to maximize their pre-tax income;
(2) all people derive satisfaction from satisfying this duty; and,
(3) all people place the same relative value on this type of satisfaction, compared with the satisfaction they get from leisure and from doing work they particularly like, as they did on personal income-consumption satisfactions in the original economy we imagined.

In this second type of economy, citizens will be motivated to respond to market signals in just the same way as in the first type of economy. Thus, people will try just as hard to keep down costs in production, just as hard to identify new areas of demand for products, and so on. However, in this second type of economy, and in contrast to the first, it will also be possible to tax all incomes at 100 per cent and redistribute them on a fully egalitarian basis without damaging the incentives people have to respond appropriately to market signals. The reason for this is that in the second type of economy people are motivated to respond to market signals by the satisfaction they get from meeting what they regard as a social duty, not by the prospect of material reward itself. Far from being an obstacle to the smooth operation of a market economy, Carens thus contends that a public-spirited work ethos (based on a social duty to maximize one's pre-tax income) can in fact provide a way of reconciling the efficiency advantages of a market system with economic equality.

However, there are some problems with the system that Carens recommends. The system posits a social duty to maximize pre-tax income. But here we return again to the question we explored above: Is it reasonable to oblige people to work in their highest-paying jobs if they have strong personal values that make them desire to work in other jobs (see Moon, 1983)? Of course, Carens's system does not in fact require people to satisfy this duty in full. The idea is that the desire to meet this duty will be just as strong – no more, no less – as the desire to acquire income and consumption goods in a conventional market economy. In our own economy, people make trade-offs between income and job satisfaction; Jones might take a job that is more satisfying, though it pays less, than another. People also make trade-offs between income and leisure; Jones decides to work only four days a week, and accept a lower salary, because she values a long weekend. In Carens's proposed system, people make similar trade-offs between social-duty satisfaction and job satisfaction and between social-duty satisfaction and leisure. However, if this is the case, in what sense is Carens really proposing a *duty* to maximize pre-tax income? Can something that is supposedly a duty be traded off against other commitments in such an open-ended way?[13]

Taking note of this problem, Martin Wilkinson has put forward an ingenious alternative to Carens's system (Wilkinson, 2000). He proposes a market economy run on the basis of what he calls the 'counterfactual duty'. This says: you have a duty to base decisions about jobs and work on what you think you would choose to do to maximize your own welfare in a world where you could keep all the income associated with different jobs, even though the income will in fact be taxed at 100 per cent and redistributed in a fully egalitarian fashion.

So, going back to the case of Clare, Wilkinson believes that Clare should ask herself: 'If I could keep all the income from being either an artist or a computer programmer, which would I choose to be?' If Clare's preferences are as we described them, then Clare will see that she should choose to be a computer programmer. For the difference in earnings between the jobs is such that, if she could keep all these earnings, she would prefer to be a computer programmer. However, in Wilkinson's proposed scheme, Clare would make this choice out of a sense of social duty, recognizing that in fact she will *not* keep the earnings from being a computer programmer. These will be taxed at a rate that may be as high as 100 per cent and redistributed to achieve a preferred egalitarian distribution. But note that in this case people do not have a duty to maximize their pre-tax incomes. If someone honestly believes that he would take a less well-paid job over a better-paid one, even if he could keep all the income associated with either job, then Wilkinson's counterfactual duty directs him to take the less well-paid job. In this way, Wilkinson avoids Carens's problem of first stipulating a social duty to maximize pre-tax income and then saying that people are free to follow or not follow the duty as much as they like.

However, there are also problems with Wilkinson's proposal. First, one might wonder whether people really could act on the proposed duty. Is it psychologically realistic to expect people to decide which job they would take, or how hard to work, if they could keep all the income from their work, when the people concerned know full well that they will not be able to keep this income? But even if this is feasible, is it reasonable to put people under such a duty? Returning to the case of Clare, does the counterfactual duty not objectionably burden her freedom of occupational choice by requiring her to work in a job that she feels brings her less close to God, without actually providing her with the income she believes is necessary to overcome this disadvantage?

In conclusion, Rawls's difference principle offers us a good rule of thumb in assessing how far inequality in reward is justified on incentives grounds. However, at least two caveats must be entered. First, we should probably adopt the principle only in a 'loose' sense, being prepared to deviate from it in cases where its strict application would bring only marginal benefits to the worst off at the price of great cost to intermediate groups. Second, not all incentive payments are strictly just merely because they are, in an immediate sense, necessary to improve the position of the worst off. The justice of incentive payments depends on the motivations that talented workers have for demanding them. In a just society, producers will share an ethos that makes them unwilling to demand incentive payments for the wrong sort of reasons (such as a desire to enjoy inequality for its own sake). Nevertheless, a society that respects individuals' freedom to pursue their own ethical projects must accept the need for some incentive payments: a case where our concern for individual liberty almost certainly does qualify the demand for economic equality.

5.5 Economic equality: a provisional summary

In closing, let us now consider what we have learnt in the last three chapters about economic inequality. The first thing to say is that it does not seem possible, in our current state of understanding, to summarize in a simple formula how much or what kind of economic inequality is fair. Indeed, it may be that it will never be possible to do this. Meritocracy captures something important, but there is good reason to doubt that it is fully fair. Luck egalitarianism helpfully corrects the main flaw in meritocracy by focusing attention on the situation of the naturally less gifted. It also contains an attractive principle of personal responsibility that is lacking in crude notions of equality of outcome. That said, we have seen how luck egalitarianism needs to be complemented by the insights of the status-power approach: a pure luck egalitarian society would likely generate intolerable social and political inequality. Incentives considerations, discussed in this chapter, also need to be factored in. This may seem a rather messy place to have reached. But our discussion has at least given us a sense of the sort of *framework* within which citizens of a moralized democracy should approach the task of identifying economic arrangements which are fair to all. Strong meritocracy; luck egalitarianism; the status-power approach; respect for reasonable incentive claims; and at least a loose priority to the worst off in judging how much inequality to tolerate on incentives grounds: these are some of the main building-blocks for a proper public discussion of economic inequality in a democratic society.

6
Equality and Difference

Right by its very nature can consist only in the application of an equal standard; but unequal individuals . . . are measurable by the same standard in so far as they are brought under the same point of view, are taken from one *definite* side only. . . . To avoid all these defects, right instead of being equal would have to be unequal.

Karl Marx, *Critique of the Gotha Programme*, 1875

The demand for equality has been understood historically as requiring that all citizens have the same rights and duties. Giving some people different rights from others has been viewed as a recipe for 'second-class citizenship'. In recent years, however, a number of critical thinkers have begun to challenge the link between equality and uniform citizenship. The critics argue that people have different interests by virtue of the different groups to which they belong, and that a 'one size fits all' approach to rights and duties is insensitive to these differences. Real, as opposed to merely formal, equality actually requires a shift to a model of *group-differentiated citizenship*, in which a citizen's rights and duties vary according to the group or groups to which she belongs. Groups are variously distinguished on the basis of gender, ethnicity, culture, religion, sexual orientation and disability.

Are the critics right? To what extent does a true society of equals require or allow for group-differentiated citizenship?

Space does not allow us to consider the arguments for group-specific rights in all contexts, but we can get a good sense of the issues involved by looking at the arguments for and against gender-, culture- and religion-specific rights (sections 6.1–6.3). In the process, we will consider whether there is a conflict between gender equality and multiculturalist demands for cultural rights. Section 6.4 briefly considers how, if at all, a frank acknowledgement of citizens' differences also requires us to recast our understanding of democracy.

6.1 Gender difference

There is an appallingly long and brutal history of inequality between men and women. Under Athenian (so-called) democracy, discussed in chapter 2, women were excluded from full citizenship. Until very recently, exclusion of women from political rights was the norm. In modern societies, including Britain, women earn less on average than men and are far from equally represented in positions of high office and top jobs (Crompton, 1997; Charles, 2002).[1] Traditional marriage law relegated wives to a position akin to chattel slavery (Mill, 1989 [1869]); until very recently in Britain, a husband could not commit the crime of rape with his wife because in law she had no right to refuse him sex. Poverty, nationally and globally, disproportionately affects women: of the 1.2 billion people in the world living on less than $1 per day, 70 per cent are women. Of the 0.9 billion people in the world who are illiterate, twice as many are women as are men (Held, 2004, p. 37). One could easily go on and on like this.

Feminism is a broad social movement which aims to challenge and overcome this persistent inequality. But how is this to be done?

We saw in chapter 2 how many philosophers who propound the natural equality of men have not extended this idea to women. The Levellers supported political rights for (most) men, but their manifestos did not advocate women's enfranchisement. Rousseau, in many ways the most egalitarian social contract theorist, excludes women from rights of political participation in his republic. Many of these thinkers tacitly accept Aristotle's model of the household as a kind of miniature kingdom in which the husband/father is the king (see section 2.1). An obvious first step in the struggle for gender equality, therefore, is to demand women's inclusion as full citizens with the same political rights as men. One of the founding texts of feminism, Mary Wollstonecraft's *A Vindication of the Rights of Woman*, contains a tentative glimpse of this idea:

> I may excite laughter, by dropping an hint, which I mean to pursue, some future time, for I really think that women ought to have representatives, instead of being arbitrarily governed without having any direct share allowed them in the deliberations of government. (Wollstonecraft, 1995 [1792], p. 237)

The demand for equal political rights emerged as a central demand of 'first-wave' feminism in the late nineteenth and early twentieth centuries. Extending this approach, feminists sought also to abolish legal restrictions on women's entry into professions, such as the legal profession, and to reform the law of marriage under which wives lost basic rights over their bodies and wealth to their husbands.

However, even if men and women have the same rights in law, they will not necessarily be equal in terms of the underlying opportunities they enjoy or the power they hold. For the law does not exist in a vacuum. It exists in a social context which structures women's opportunities and expectations in definite ways, and equality in law does not of itself correct or abolish the disadvantages that result from this. Particularly important here is women's historic role as primary, unpaid care-givers within households, a role that they still largely retain (Charles, 2002, pp. 70–2). This care-giving role consumes energy and time, and means that many women do not compete on a level playing field with similarly talented men in employment. By reducing their employability, this role also contributes to women's financial dependency on men which, in turn, is a source of unequal power within the household (Okin, 1989, pp. 134–69). The pressures of care-giving may also diminish women's opportunity for political participation. The basic problem is that many institutions in the public sphere, including those of employment and active citizenship, have been traditionally the sphere of men who had few, if any, caring responsibilities, and these institutions remain geared to that traditional male norm.

In light of this social context, some argue that what women need is not only strictly equal or identical rights to men in areas of historic exclusion, but also some gender-specific rights that, by taking account of women's particular circumstances, achieve more effective equality. Many feminists in the United States campaigned in the early twentieth century for special legal protections for women wage workers. The campaigners argued that women were in a much weaker position to bargain for limits on working hours than men due to the fact they had fewer employment opportunities and were less unionized. Given these gender-specific disadvantages, they argued that the state should regulate women's working hours even if it did not regulate men's (Rhode, 1998 [1992], pp. 346–7). Historically, some feminists have argued that the objective is not to end the gendered division of care work in itself (at least not in the immediate future), but rather to enable women to perform their role as primary care workers without being rendered dependent on and unequal to men. 'Difference' in social roles and expectations is not itself the immediate problem; the problem is the inequality in opportunity, status and power to which it has historically led. Detaching 'difference' from inequality might require a range of gender-specific entitlements ranging from labour laws such as those just noted to paying mothers a social wage to reflect the work they do as carers (Rathbone, 1924).

A quite different perspective holds that real equality with men is not achievable without taking a critical stance towards the traditional gendered division of care work itself. This is connected with one of the key slogans of feminism's 'second wave', which dates from the 1960s, that the 'personal is political'. Feminist critics argue that mainstream theories of justice, such as that of Rawls (see chapter 5), fail to extend their insights into the family sphere (Okin, 1989, pp. 89–109). But the family should not be treated as part of a private realm outside the scope of the demand for equality. How the family is arranged impacts far too much on the public realms of employment and citizenship for it to be treated in this way. Fair family arrangements will spread care responsibilities much more evenly between men and women in order to enable their equal participation in the public sphere. The guiding vision is the transcendence of 'difference' in a 'humanist' society in which men and women on average perform pretty much the same social roles. As Susan Moller Okin describes it:

> A just future would be one without gender. In its social structures and practices, one's sex would have no more relevance than one's eye color or the length of one's toes. No assumptions would be made about "male" and "female" roles; childbearing would be so conceptually separated from child rearing and other family responsibilities that it would be a cause for surprise, and no little concern, if men and women were not equally responsible for domestic life or if children were to spend much more time with one parent than the other. It would be a future in which men and women participated in more or less equal numbers in every sphere of life, from infant care to different kinds of paid work to high-level politics. (Okin, 1989, p. 171)

For those who endorse this humanist perspective, the strategy of gender-specific rights has clear dangers. Precisely by recognizing existing gender difference, the strategy might work to consolidate it. For example, if employers are required to grant women rights to childcare leave, over and above those for male employees, then this may serve to consolidate the underlying inequality between men and women in the assumption of care responsibilities. Such an approach may lead 'to the establishment of special "mummy tracks" that often turn into mummy traps' (Rhode, 1998 [1992], p. 349). From the humanist perspective, it is better to work to reform institutions in the public sphere so that they can accommodate all those who carry primary care responsibilities, whether male or female. So it is important to press for parental leave arrangements for employees, but to demand significant leave entitlement for male as well as female workers. This will enable men and women to share in care responsibilities in the home while also both retaining a strong presence in the public sphere. This amounts to 'a "dynamic" approach to sexual difference [which] recognise[s] that although gender-specific responsibilities and needs exist, many of these can in principle become gender neutral' (Bryson, 1999, pp. 77–8).

From a liberal or multiculturalist point of view, however, the humanist emphasis on reforming family life might seem oppressive. If an adult man and woman subscribe to a religion which asserts a woman's place to be in the home, shouldn't they be free to act on their beliefs? In response it will be said that few (if any) feminists think that the state should prohibit this. They do not envisage that the state will require all households to submit to inspections and keep records to show that domestic responsibilities are being equally shared. The state's basic role is rather to ensure that basic institutions, such as employment, are not structured (as they often currently are) in a way that strongly discourages more egalitarian family models, and that all individuals, men and women, have real choice about the kind of family arrangements they form. But this response may be a little too slick. Granted that the state should not mandate egalitarian family arrangements, should it at least encourage them, e.g., through publicly funded campaigns that encourage men to take a more equal share of care responsibilities? While this would not be anything like as oppressive as prohibiting traditional family arrangements, it would nevertheless send a clear message to some religious and cultural groups that the community regards their ways of life as less legitimate than others. Is this a message that the state should send out? The idea that the 'personal is political' is a valuable one in that it puts a spotlight on inequalities that have been left hidden in the past. But it also clearly raises some tough questions about how and the extent to which the state should show respect for diverse lifestyles, an issue to which we shall return when we look at multiculturalism further below.

Putting this issue to one side for now, we have seen that the humanist perspective gives us reason to be somewhat wary of gender-specific rights, but does this mean there is no place at all for such rights? In replying, we should note first that not all gender difference is rooted in social structures. While there may be nothing in nature which dictates that women rather than men rear children, pregnancy is (at present) another matter. As a matter of biology (at present) it is women who bear babies to term. In the United States, some feminists have argued that by virtue of this, women employees should have a gender-specific right to pregnancy leave. However, the demand is controversial because it contradicts the idea that if the law is to be non-discriminatory, and hence fair, it must be 'gender-blind', giving the same rights to men and women. Giving special rights to women looks, on this view, like discrimination against men (Minow, 1990; Bryson, 1999, pp. 74–5). However, the example of pregnancy surely shows just how odd it is in fact to equate fairness with gender-blindness in the law. The egalitarian theories of fairness we examined in chapter 4, such as Dworkin's theory of equality of resources, assert that we should design our institutions and policies so that people are not significantly disadvantaged relative to others due to differences in their natural endowments. It is this basic principle which explains why egalitarians support taxation of talented workers for the benefit of the less talented and transfers to those who suffer disabilities. A policy of granting women more employment leave than men to cover pregnancy is simply another expression of this basic principle. It protects women against potential disadvantage in employment stemming from a specific natural endowment that women typically have, and which only women have: a capacity to carry babies to term. Complaining that a gender-specific right to pregnancy leave is unfair 'special treatment' is about as sensible as complaining that a subsidy to help people with impaired mobility to buy wheelchairs is unfair special treatment (which is to say that it is really not sensible at all).

Some gender-specific rights might also be defended as offering possible *means of transition* to a more humanist society. A humanist society requires a radical redesign of institutions to enable people to balance institutional and family responsibilities. Given that it is women who currently suffer most acutely from imbalances between these responsibilities, one can plausibly argue (though the claim requires investigation) that the necessary reforms are more likely to occur if women are in a position to influence policy in our major institutions. Gender-specific rights that fall under the rubric of 'affirmative action' might then be defended as a means of getting women into top positions so as to effect more rapid change. In the political context, such policies may take the form of reserving a proportion of seats in assemblies for women, or having women-only short-lists for the selection of a party's candidates for elections (Phillips, 1995, pp. 57–83).

Finally, there is the point that until such time as institutions like the family have evolved so that we have a humanist society, many women will derive great benefit from some gender-specific rights, in areas like employment and social welfare, that compensate for the disadvantage caused by traditional institutions. Even if such rights work to slow the transition to a more humanist society, a balance must be struck between the interest of future women (and men) in living in a humanist society and the interest of today's women in living a decent life in a non-humanist society.

6.2 Cultural difference

'Multiculturalism' as a term refers both to the fact of cultural diversity in a society and to a type of politics which demands group-specific rights aimed at the recognition and protection of minority cultures. These might include rights of self-government for the minority within an area or with respect to a set of issues; special rights of political representation in wider decision-making bodies; rights of subsidy and support; or exemptions from specific laws or policies (Kymlicka, 1995, pp. 26–33). Amongst egalitarians, multiculturalism in this second, political sense is very controversial. Some argue that it represents a necessary development of the demand for equality (Young, 1989, 1990; Taylor, 1992; Kymlicka, 1989, 1995).[2] Others regard it as a reactionary movement which threatens to reverse progress towards genuine equality (Okin, 1999; Barry, 2000). In this section we will look at some general arguments surrounding multiculturalism before addressing the specific debate about exemption rights in the following section.

Multiculturalists appeal to equality. They point out a way or ways in which membership of a minority culture can put one at a disadvantage relative to members of society's mainstream culture. They argue that group-specific rights are necessary to address this disadvantage. However, amongst multiculturalists there are different accounts of the nature of the disadvantage which creates the need for group-specific rights and of the kind of group-specific rights which are desirable.[3]

According to one very influential argument developed by Will Kymlicka, one of the key interests at stake is the individual's interest in *autonomy*, in being able to reflect in a critical and informed way on our values and goals and choose our 'plan of life'. To exercise autonomy, we need a 'context of choice' to provide a menu of meaningful life options. This is provided by our 'societal culture' (Kymlicka, 1995, pp. 82–4). Now nations such as the United States and Canada contain aboriginal peoples and other minorities (such as the Quebecois) with distinct cultures from mainstream anglophone culture. Their cultures are at risk of being overwhelmed. Were these cultures to disappear, members of these groups would lose the context of choice in which they exercise their autonomy. Their ability to function as autonomous beings would be jeopardized. To prevent this, group-specific rights, such as rights of self-government within particular areas, are essential (Kymlicka, 1995, pp. 108–15). Kymlicka refines this argument in two ways. First, he distinguishes group-specific rights that provide 'external protections' against assimilation from rights that allow authorities within minority cultural groups to place 'internal restrictions' on the freedom of their own members (Kymlicka, 1995, pp. 35–44). Kymlicka regards internal restrictions as illegitimate in principle because they conflict with a concern for individual autonomy.[4] Second, Kymlicka distinguishes the case of aboriginal peoples from that of immigrants. Immigrants *choose* to uproot themselves from their culture of origin and move to a society with a different culture. Because of this, they cannot claim the same right to the protection of their societal culture as aboriginal peoples (Kymlicka, 1995, pp. 95–8).

How successful is Kymlicka's argument from autonomy for culture-protecting group-specific rights? An obvious challenge to Kymlicka's argument is: Why do people necessarily need the context of choice provided by their original 'societal culture'? If that culture is disappearing over time, will they not simply find a new context of choice in the mainstream culture? In reply, Kymlicka contends that it is difficult and costly to make the transition to a new societal culture. However, if such a transition is possible for immigrants, as Kymlicka assumes, then presumably it is possible for aboriginal peoples. The transition is indeed likely to involve costs, for example, the costs of time, energy and resources involved in becoming more fluent in a dominant language. But the state can assist with these costs (for example, by paying for language classess and, perhaps, compensating members of the minority group for the opportunity costs of taking these classes). As long as we are concerned only with the need for *a* context of choice it is hard to see why culture-protecting rights are necessarily to be preferred to this alternative policy of assisted transition to the mainstream culture. Indeed, if this culture is more open and diverse than the original culture, perhaps the autonomy of people in the minority group will be enhanced by such a transition, giving us reason to prefer this alternative (see Waldron, 1995, for further discussion).[5]

Another account of multiculturalism appeals to a concept we referred to briefly in chapter 4, that of *recognition* (Taylor, 1992; see also Fraser, 1995). In an influential essay, Charles Taylor distinguishes two forms of recognition. In the first instance, all people warrant recognition and respect simply as human beings. This is expressed, for example, in doctrines of human rights. But people do not demand recognition simply as human beings and bearers of general human interests. They also demand recognition as members of particular cultural groups, as bearers of specific cultures and ways of life. The intuition might be usefully recast in terms of Rawls's idea that justice must concern itself not only with liberty, income and wealth, but also with the conditions for people to enjoy self-respect. The multiculturalist claims that one's self-respect is tied up with the recognition of one's culture: if my ethnic and/or religious culture is not publicly recognized and affirmed by my society, then I will suffer diminished self-respect. Public recognition should take the form of group-specific rights that acknowledge, affirm and protect my ethnic and/or religious culture. Note that if self-respect is a condition for effective autonomy, then this can also be seen as a kind of autonomy argument for multiculturalism.

In societies like our own, members of aboriginal and immigrant cultural minorities are often victims of status inequality and this might well be detrimental to their self-respect. Some kind of public affirmation of aboriginal and immigrant cultures might be helpful to correct this. Nevertheless, there are some reasons to be circumspect about this proposed 'politics of recognition'. First, as Brian Barry notes, calls on the state to affirm (rather than simply tolerate) different cultures and lifestyles easily fall into incoherence (Barry, 2000, pp. 270–1). It is hard, for example, to see how the state could simultaneously affirm a minority religious identity which condemns homosexuality, and a culture which celebrates gay, lesbian and queer sexualities.

Second, as Taylor notes, what many cultural groups demand are 'measures designed to ensure survival [of their culture] through indefinite future generations' (Taylor, 1992, p. 41, note 16). People want group-specific rights that will ensure not only that they continue to live in their culture (Kymlicka's concern), but that the culture survives for their children, and their children's children, and so on. Now the most effective way to ensure one's culture's survival for 'indefinite future generations' is to impose what Kymlicka calls 'internal restrictions' on group members. For example, a group might be given rights of self-government under which their internal authorities can impose penalties on members who break with the group's traditions and beliefs, as is the case with some Native American groups in the United States. However, as Kymlicka warns, group rights of this kind clearly violate the autonomy of individual group members. Far from being a support to autonomy, in this sort of case the politics of recognition looks like a threat to autonomy.

A further, related concern relates to the position of women. Susan Moller Okin argues that many of the cultures that are candidates for group-specific, culture-protecting rights are deeply sexist, sanctioning much more severe forms of women's subordination than is practised in the mainstream cultures of liberal democratic societies (Okin, 1999). There is, she contends, a real danger that special rights aimed at protecting and accommodating these cultures could threaten women's interests. She cites as an example the attempt to use men's cultural background as an extenuating factor in cases where men are guilty of violent crimes against women. A very similar point also applies to people of gay, lesbian and queer sexualities. Many traditional cultures condemn these sexualities. So there is an issue as to whether the granting of special rights to protect and accommodate these cultures might consolidate the oppression of people in these cultures with these sexualities.

In thinking about how a multiculturalist might reply to some of these criticisms, and in particular that of feminists like Okin, it may help to take note of an important topic of feminist discussion that we bracketed earlier. Our discussion in section 6.1 focused on gender difference. But since the 1980s (if not before) feminists have also been engaged in a discussion of 'difference' as it applies to women as a group. Black feminists, such as bell hooks, have argued that the mainstream feminist model of womanhood and women's interests has been based on an overgeneralization from the experience of white (also middle-class, also heterosexual) women (hooks, 1981, 2000; Spelman, 1988). But the shape of disadvantage clearly differs along dimensions of ethnicity, class and sexual orientation in ways that make it questionable as to whether women of a specific ethnicity, class or sexual orientation, in describing how they are oppressed as women, can claim to speak for all women:

> White women who dominate feminist discourse, who for the most part make and articulate feminist theory, have little or no understanding of white supremacy as a racial politic, of the psychological impact of class, of their political status within a racist, sexist, capitalist state. (hooks, 2000, p. 4)

The implication is that the feminist movement needs to be sensitive to the heterogeneity in its ranks. The movement must be conceived coalitionally, as a site of ongoing discussion and negotiation between those with different experiences of oppression, not as a simple unitary uprising against a uniform 'common oppression'. This is an important point to make in its own right. In the form of this critique of mainstream feminism, moreover, one can also begin to see the form of a possible reply that a multiculturalist might make to feminists like Okin. (This is not to imply that black feminist critics of mainstream feminism like hooks would necessarily agree with such a reply.) Do feminists like Okin fall into the trap of understating the degree of actual and legitimate difference amongst women? Are they, the critic will ask, presenting *a* reasonable conception of women's interests as *the only* reasonable conception, ignoring the extent to which ideas of gender equality are themselves subject to some degree of reasonable variation across cultures (Parekh, 1999, 2000)? Is this another case of white, middle-class, Western women objectionably conflating their interests or values with those of women as a whole? This is certainly one of the claims that defenders of multiculturalism have made in response to critiques like Okin's. Sander Gilman comments:

> Okin claims that 'women' are the prime victims of religious practice. But can one really speak of 'women' as a unitary category? Her representation of 'woman' as a singular, monolithic category is difficult to understand at the close of the millennium. . . . women are unquestionably a diverse group, as feminists have argued for over a decade. The very claim that Western (or Westernized), bourgeois (and, yes, white) women can speak for all women was exploded in discussions within and beyond the United Nations meeting on the status of women held at Nairobi more than a decade ago. (Gilman, 1999, p. 55)

In a similar vein, Azizah Al-Hibri points out that 'many contemporary women with established careers have adopted the Orthodox or Hasidic Jewish way of life as adults. . . . It is hard . . . to argue that these accomplished women have been so misled as to choose an oppressive lifestyle. There is something condescending, even patriarchal, about such a claim' (Al-Hibri, 1999, p. 44).

In reply, one can point out that while some women make such choices in an informed manner, from a position of independence, this is not necessarily true for all women who lead these lifestyles. Some might feel the practices as an unwelcome imposition. Moreover, even if some women do endorse such lifestyles, we should remember 'that persons subjected to unjust conditions often adapt their preferences so as to conceal the injustice of their situation from themselves' (Okin, 1999, p. 126). In other words, if there is a danger that feminists like Okin may underestimate legitimate cultural difference in the shape of gender equality, there is no less a danger that multiculturalists may romanticize women's acceptance of cultural or religiously sanctioned practices. Recall: 'Slaves in their chains lose everything, even their desire to be free' (Rousseau, 1994 [1762], book 1, chapter 4).

6.3   The exemptions debate

One particular issue prompted by multiculturalist politics concerns whether members of religious or cultural minorities should receive exemptions from laws that place a distinctively heavy burden on them. In Britain, for example, turban-wearing Sikhs have an exemption from wearing a helmet when riding a motorbike, and laws regulating the slaughter of livestock include an exemption allowing Jews and Muslims to slaughter according to the requirements of their faiths (Barry, 2000, pp. 40–50). In the United States, there is a long history of campaigns by religious groups to win exemptions from laws that place a distinctive burden on them. One recent case, Oregon *vs.* Smith, concerned whether Native Americans had the right to use the drug peyote in religious rituals in contravention of anti-drug laws.[6] Should governments grant such exemptions? Do they conflict with the idea that the state should show equal concern and respect to its members? Or do they in fact express this very idea?

Let's start with the exemption from helmet laws for Sikhs. The government passes a law requiring citizens to wear helmets when riding motorbikes. Turban-wearing Sikhs cannot ride motorbikes and satisfy this law. Thus, so the argument goes, they lose the opportunity to ride motorbikes. By granting Sikhs an exemption, they retain the same opportunity to ride motorbikes as others. The exemption means that there is a difference in the rights of Sikhs and others. But, so it is argued, this helps to maintain an underlying equality in opportunities between Sikhs and other citizens. A strict legal equality is being suspended in the interests of preserving a higher equality in opportunities. As Bhiku Parekh puts it, speaking about a similar exemption: 'the [legal] inequality grows out of the requirements of the principle of equal respect for all, and is not so much inequality as an appropriate translation of that principle in a different religious context' (Parekh, 1997, p. 135).

However, as Brian Barry points out, all laws burden some people more than others: 'Speed limits inhibit only those who like to drive fast. Laws prohibiting drunk-driving have no impact on teetotallers. Only smokers are stopped by prohibitions on smoking in public places. . . . This is simply how things are' (Barry, 2000, p. 34). What, the critic might ask, is so different about the burden suffered by Sikhs under the helmet law? Why does it require that an exemption be given, when there are so many other cases of differential burdening in which we would not say that the burdened should get exemptions? It is, moreover, quite wrong to argue that, in view of the helmet law, Sikhs have less opportunity than others. This claim rests on the view that the opportunities open to a person are affected by the beliefs or preferences she has (Barry, 2000, p. 37). But this view is clearly incorrect. If Edward and Freda are legally free to go to the zoo, and each can afford the price of admission, then they both have the opportunity to go to the zoo. The fact that Freda's religion forbids her to watch animals in captivity means that she is less willing to make use of this opportunity than Edward is; but it does not mean that she somehow ceases to have the opportunity. Similarly with Sikhs under the helmet law. They have the opportunity to ride a motorbike, provided they wear a helmet, like anyone else. The fact that their religion makes it hard to wear a helmet does not mean they lose the opportunity that others have. They will just be less willing to make use of it.

In light of Barry's forceful criticisms, is it possible to make a case for religious and culturally based exemptions from general laws? One possible line of defence is to employ a device like Rawls's 'original position' (see section 5.2). Imagine that in selecting the basic principles of justice to regulate their society, the parties in the original position are asked to consider how their society should respond to situations in which members of a particular religion are distinctively burdened by a law. The parties have to consider this question behind the 'veil of ignorance', not knowing what religion they will have in society and, thus, what the likelihood is that they will be burdened in this way. But they understand that this is a possibility. How would the parties in this original position respond to this issue?

On the one hand, they will clearly be concerned to ensure that laws are generally respected. This will make them circumspect about endorsing a principle that requires or allows a lot of exemptions. On the other hand, they will appreciate the risk involved in endorsing a principle that permits no exemptions; after all, they could find themselves in the position of someone who is seriously burdened by a law by virtue of their religion. Balancing these two concerns, the parties would perhaps seek an intermediate position: the state should grant exemptions where a law bears heavily on the practices of a given religion and where the exemption does not allow people to violate the basic interests of others (and also, perhaps, to put their own lives and freedoms at serious risk). Let's call this the *balancing approach* to exemptions. This approach has been very influential in the United States. Lawyers and philosophers have argued that under the nation's constitutional guarantee of 'free exercise' of religion, laws may not place a 'substantial burden' on freedom to pursue one's religion unless the restriction serves a 'compelling state interest' and is the least burdensome way of securing this interest (Nussbaum, 1999, pp. 111–12). Exactly what counts as a compelling state interest under the balancing approach is a matter of dispute, but most would agree that compelling state interests include such things as citizens' interests in life, physical integrity and in receiving an education adequate to be able to function as a citizen outside of any particular religious group.[7] So, as practised in the United States, the balancing approach does not – or should not – permit exemptions that would threaten these interests. However, one can, for example, make a good case under the approach for granting the Native American Church an exemption from anti-drug laws to permit the use of peyote in religious rituals (Freeman, 2002, pp. 22–5).

Supporters of the balancing approach do face some tough questions, however – questions that might give the parties in the original position reason to pause before endorsing it. In particular, we should surely insist that any exemptions regime respect a principle of equity: that like cases be treated alike. While this sounds like an innocuous requirement, in fact it is likely to create real problems for the balancing approach in practice.

Consider first the problem of equity as between two or more religious groups who are burdened in similar ways by a given law. If we grant an exemption to one, we should grant it to the other(s). For instance, if Sikhs are allowed to carry knives in public places as an expression of their religion, then perhaps self-styled Druids should be allowed to carry sickles or small swords for the same reason (Barry, 2000, pp. 50–4). However, as we extend the exemption to more groups, its very desirability is called into question. Laws against carrying knives in public exist to increase our physical security. Granting an exemption to one, relatively small, religious group may not put this important objective at risk. But if we extend the exemption to more groups there will come a point at which the objectives of the law are compromised. In seeking to be fair to different religious groups in the granting of an exemption we may have to extend the exemption to so many people that it becomes undesirable to grant an exemption at all.

This possibility is made even more likely by the need to ensure equity between religious and non-religious citizens. Many citizens are not religious, but do have serious, deeply felt ethical beliefs that can cause them to be distinctively burdened by laws. It is not fair to refuse them exemptions if we grant exemptions for religious citizens (Smith, 1998; Galston, 2004, pp. 66–9). Once again, though, if we extend exemptions in this way, we might undermine the goals that a given law exists to promote, making it undesirable to grant an exemption at all.

There is, in addition, the practical problem of determining whether someone's ethical grounds for an exemption are sincere and serious enough to make it worth considering whether an exemption is due. Deciding what counts as a religion is hard enough. Deciding what counts as a serious ethical system, religious or not, is even harder. Does the Hell's Angel who demands an exemption from motorbike helmet laws have a serious ethical position that warrants the same consideration as that we give to the Sikh? Indeed, it is worth reflecting on the full range of questions that we face when an individual presses an exemption claim (see Greenawalt, 2000, for a related discussion). Does the individual have a genuine religion or ethical system? How seriously does the law burden the individual's pursuit of her religion or ethical system? Are the interests protected by the law too important to justify granting an exemption at all? Are there other groups who are burdened by the law in a similar way? Would the objectives of the law be compromised if the exemption were extended to these other groups, as well as to the group of the individual now demanding the exemption? In many cases, these are hard questions and reasonable people will disagree about the answers. As a result, there is a clear danger that the pattern of exemptions that emerges from legislative or judicial decision-making will lack consistency and, hence, legitimacy in the eyes of the citizen. Concerns of this kind underlay the United State's Supreme Court's decision in Oregon *vs.* Smith that courts got out of the exemptions business, though the ruling did not question the right of legislatures to craft exemptions (Barry, 2000, pp. 171–3).

In short, then, one can make a case that fairness requires exemptions, subject to certain conditions; but these conditions should include an equity condition (like cases treated alike). This condition would probably reduce the number of justifiable exemptions, and it would be demanding and controversial to live up to it in practice.

In closing this discussion of multiculturalism, it is important to emphasize that our concern has been with group-specific rights that *differentiate* a cultural or religious group from others. However, this is not necessarily the issue at the heart of every multiculturalism controversy. Consider, for example, the argument in France about whether Muslim girls should be allowed to wear a headscarf, the *hijab*, to state schools. The issue here is not clearly about a special right, an exemption of some kind. The girls can argue that all citizens have a right to freedom of religion and that this implies a right on the part of all children to wear things to school that are expressive of their faith. The demand to be allowed to wear the *hijab* is not a demand for special treatment, but a demand to be allowed to do what all children should have a right to do. Of course, there is another side to the argument.

Some feminists argue that the *hijab* is a symbol of women's oppression and that state schools should therefore prohibit it in the interests of gender equality. However, this is perhaps precisely the sort of case in which some feminists risk understating the compatibility of different cultural or religious forms with gender equality. And even if one agrees with these feminist critics, my purpose is not so much to press the claim of these Muslim girls as to point out that, regardless of how far one agrees with them, they are pressing a claim for a universal, not a group-specific, right.

6.4 Democracy revisited

Chapter 2 presented the ideal of a moralized democracy in which citizens seek to make laws based on an assessment of what they think is fair to all. We noted how citizens might use social contract thought-experiments, of the kind employed by Rawls, to help frame their deliberations about what is fair. However, some supporters of the 'politics of difference' argue that this model of impartial reasoning in politics carries great dangers to the disadvantaged. Iris Marion Young, an influential proponent of this view, writes: 'In a society where some groups are privileged while others are oppressed, insisting that as citizens persons should leave behind their particular affiliations and experiences to adopt a general point of view serves only to reinforce the privilege' (Young, 1989, p. 257).

I think what Young has in mind here is something like this. If society is already divided into haves and have-nots, oppressors and oppressed, then a call to take everyone's interests into account seems to undercut the possibility of a radical critique of existing inequality. Proposals that challenge the underlying inequality can be characterized as objectionably partial: as benefitting one group (the poor, say) at the expense of the other (the rich, say), as selfish 'class legislation'. Young argues that instead of calling on citizens to be impartial, we should seek to redress power imbalances within the political system so that the disadvantaged can more effectively advance their interests. Disadvantaged groups should receive state support to organize themselves 'so that they gain a sense of collective empowerment'. They should have protected rights to voice a group analysis of policy proposals, combined with corresponding duties on the part of policy-makers 'to show that they have taken these perspectives into consideration'. They should even have a 'veto power regarding specific policies that affect a group directly' (Young, 1989, pp. 261–2).

Young's critique of the 'ideal of impartiality' is overstated. First, it is important to be clear that the kind of impartiality that is recommended by thinkers such as Rawls and Dworkin does not take existing inequalities in wealth, power and so on in our society as given. The idea is not to take the status quo as our baseline and to ask what makes everyone better off starting from this baseline. Genuine impartiality consists precisely in our ability to detach ourselves from the status quo and ask whether its *constitutive* inequalities can themselves be justified. That is the point of social contract thought-experiments such as Rawls's original position (section 5.2). To this, Young points out that whatever the aspiration behind the ideal of impartiality, the fact is that we are all limited in our ability to be impartial. Just look at Rawls, the critic might say. Haven't we already noted the feminist criticism that Rawls develops his theory of justice in a way that ignores what is going on inside the family, thereby ignoring basic causes of gender inequality rooted in the division of care responsibilities (Okin, 1989, pp. 89–109)?

Putting the specific issue of Rawls's treatment of the family to one side,[8] Young is surely right to point to the fallibility of citizens as moral agents, seeking to be fair to all. No matter how hard we try, all of us at some point are likely to fail to appreciate just how the shoe pinches for other people. Moreover, starting as we do from a society in which there are severe inequalities, it would be very naive to think that a large degree of self-interested bias will not creep into the deliberations of richer, more powerful people. They might well feel no strong motivation to be impartial at all. For these reasons, Young's basic recommendation, that our system of political representation should contain measures to enhance the voice and power of disadvantaged groups, is compelling. It is consistent with the argument we have already noted in section

6.1 for enhancing the presence of women in political bodies, an argument which can be extended, for example, to cultural and religious minorities. It is consistent, too, with efforts to promote organizations like trade unions to give greater voice to those who currently live primarily by the sale of labour-power (Cohen and Rogers, 1995a; White, 1998). Many further examples could doubtless be added.

However, the point of such measures is surely to help us, as a democratic community, do better at meeting the demands of the impartial perspective: we are getting all voices to the table, and into the proverbial corridors of power, so that final decisions more truly track what fairness, impartially considered, requires. To this extent, Young's basic recommendation seems to rest on precisely the ideal of impartiality that she wants to reject. Her tacit reliance on this ideal can be seen in another way. In the kind of political process that Young proposes, where group representation plays a substantial role, how are members of one group meant to respond to the demands made by others? How do groups decide what they can rightfully claim from others before they issue demands? Will various groups simply appeal to their own self-interest without concern for the welfare of others? This is not what Young seems to envisage: 'In a democratically structured public where social inequality is mitigated through group representation, individuals or groups cannot simply assert that they want something; they must say that justice requires or allows that they have it' (Young, 1989, p. 263; also 1990, pp. 118–19). But will this not require them to try to look at the situation of themselves and others in an impartial way? Of course, they may fail. But if democratic politics is not to reduce to a clash of self-interest, the point is surely to try.

7
The Future of Equality

Equality, it is said, is a theorists' vision, which cannot exist
in practice. But if an abuse is inevitable, does it follow
that it should not at least be controlled? It is precisely
because the force of things always tends to destroy
equality that the force of the law should always tend to
conserve it.

Jean-Jacques Rousseau, *The Social Contract*, 1762

In the course of this book, we have looked in-depth at the
content, justification and desirability of the demand for
equality. Interesting though this might be as an intellectual
exercise, some will question whether the exercise has any
practical point. Many will claim that the politics of equality
has now run its course. Three decades ago, politicians who
opposed moves towards greater equality (specifically, economic equality) still felt obliged to explain why they opposed
it. In the first decades of the twenty-first century, hardly any
politician in Britain or the United States speaks about equality. It is a real question as to whether the demand for equality, particularly in the economy, will shape national politics
in the future as it has done in the past (though it would be
wrong to assume that there has ever been a golden age of
equality politics from which we have now fallen). On the
other hand, one might argue that equality politics is in fact

gaining a new lease of life at the global level. When the leaders of the world's largest economies gather at summits of the G8, they are now routinely accompanied by large numbers of protestors, and while the protestors are motivated by many concerns, the stark inequality between rich and poor nations is certainly one of them. Are the protestors right to think that the demand for equality applies at a global level? And, within the national context, is it likely that ideas of the kind discussed in this book can still achieve any purchase? Or is equality passé?

Section 7.1 explores the first of these questions. Inequalities across nations raise not only practical but basic philosophical questions: To what extent are citizens of rich societies obliged to act to reduce the inequality between themselves and people in poor societies? Do the principles regulating economic equality, discussed in chapters 3 through 6, apply only within nation-states, or do they apply at the global level? Sections 7.2 and 7.3 then present cases respectively for and against the continuing relevance of equality politics at the national level. The pessimist's case, set out in section 7.2, offers some reasons for thinking that, within the nation-state, equality looks like an increasingly utopian demand that is unlikely to get any purchase (in part because of the pressures created by 'globalization'). The optimist's case, set out in section 7.3, offers some reasons for thinking that equality politics can retain its relevance.

7.1   Must equality go global?

Economic inequalities within nations like Britain and the United States are considerable. But global inequalities are even more severe. Over 20 per cent of the world's population in 1998 were living below the World Bank's official measure of extreme poverty (living on roughly $1 per day or less). The rich societies comprising 14.9 per cent of the world's population enjoy almost 80 per cent of world income. The poorest 20 per cent on the planet collectively enjoy a mere one-third of 1 per cent of world income (Pogge, 2002, pp. 97–9). If we look at wealth rather than income, we find that '[t]he assets of the top three billionaires in the world are more than the combined GNP of all least developed countries and their 600 million people' (United Nations Development Programme, 1999, p. 3, cited in Pogge, 2002, p. 99). These figures are staggering. The reality they describe has provoked the emergence of a whole new social movement around the world which aims to reform or abolish the global economic order that is allegedly responsible for them (Kingsnorth, 2003). The figures suggest (though in themselves they do not necessarily entail) that there is a massive injustice at the global level and that people in rich societies have urgent obligations to act to improve the position of the global poor.

Yet, while it seems undeniable on the face of it that people in rich societies have obligations of some sort, it is not so clear exactly how we should characterize these obligations. The theoretical discussion of economic equality reviewed in chapters 3 to 6 assumes the nation-state as its context. Is this merely a simplifying assumption that we should now relax? Does the demand for equality in fact apply at the global level rather than simply at the national level? Are obligations to act to improve the position of the global poor grounded in precisely the same considerations of fairness that we have discussed in a national context?

One way of getting at the basic issues at the heart of this debate is to consider the views of John Rawls, whose work, as we have seen, has inspired so much recent work on equality and fairness. Intriguingly, Rawls firmly rejects the view that egalitarian principles of the kind he defends for the domestic case should also apply at the international level (Rawls, 1999b). Rawls posits a world divided into distinct 'peoples' with their respective states. He imagines representatives of these peoples in an original position in which they are to agree a set of principles to regulate their interaction. As in the original position he imagines for the domestic context, the parties are behind a veil of ignorance. They do not know 'the size of the territory, or the population, or the relative strength of the people whose fundamental interests they represent' (Rawls, 1999b, p. 32). The parties take as the 'fundamental interests' of their peoples their interest in maintaining independence and in their ability to achieve justice domestically. Let us refer to this as the *original position of the peoples* (OPP). Situated in the OPP, Rawls argues that the peoples' representatives will select certain 'familiar and traditional principles of justice' to regulate their interaction. In the first instance, Rawls imagines the peoples in the OPP to be liberal peoples (peoples committed to liberal political values internally), but he extends the discussion to include what he calls 'decent hierarchical' peoples, and he claims that these peoples would choose essentially the same principles for the international order.

With respect to preventing global poverty or inequality, what principles would peoples' representatives choose in the OPP? The reader will recall that, in the domestic version of the original position, the parties select a difference principle to regulate economic inequality: inequality is fair only if it works to benefit the group that is worst off under the inequality (see section 5.2). In the international sphere, however, Rawls claims that the OPP representatives will select a much more limited principle: 'Peoples have a duty to assist other peoples living under unfavorable conditions that prevent their having a just or decent political and social regime' (Rawls, 1999b, p. 37). Acting on this 'duty of assistance' in a world like our own will likely reduce the appalling degree of inequality. But it is important to see that the duty in itself is not egalitarian in motivation. The idea is not to assist poorer peoples so as to mitigate inequality between peoples for its own sake, but only so as to enable these peoples to achieve a stable domestic order that meets certain basic moral standards. A domestic parallel would be policies aimed to rehabilitate drug addicts and the homeless into mainstream society. Such policies might well temper the inequalities within a nation, but clearly one does not have to believe in limiting inequality for its own sake to support them; one need only think that everyone ought to be able to lead at least a minimally decent life. In Rawls's 'Law of Peoples' there is in fact no principle to regulate economic inequalities between peoples as such. Rawls's view is that *outside the nation-state, economic inequality, in itself, does not stand in need of justification by reference to principle(s) of fairness.*

Rawls's position has been challenged by critics on a number of grounds. We can distinguish two basic standpoints from which one might defend a more egalitarian account of justice at the international or global level:

1. *The radical challenge.* According to the first, radical challenge, Rawls goes awry right at the start in positing a world divided into distinct peoples (Kuper, 2000). We should start from the idea that humanity is a single moral community in which each individual has equal standing. This suggests a very different way of applying Rawls's social contract approach at the global level. As we have seen, Rawls imagines two social contracts based on two distinct 'original positions': there is, firstly, the original position to determine principles of justice to govern a (liberal) people internally; then, secondly, we imagine the OPP in which representatives of peoples come together to agree a Law of Peoples. But if humanity is a single moral community, then an obvious alternative is simply to amend Rawls's first original position. We can imagine that people in the first original position are deprived of information not only about their social class, natural talent and religion, as Rawls suggests, but also of their nationality. They are to choose principles to regulate the global economic order, not knowing whether they will be born into, as it were, 'rich Western' or 'poor Southern' countries. One might call this the *original position of global individuals* (OPGI).

Now the principles chosen in the OPGI might well be very much more egalitarian than the duty of assistance that Rawls advocates as part of his Law of Peoples. Not knowing what sort of society they will be born into, the parties in the OPGI might seek to protect the interests of themselves and their loved ones by selecting something like the difference principle (see chapter 5), but with application at the level of humanity as a whole: world economic inequality is justified only insofar as it maximizes the prospects of the globally worst-off group (Barry, 1973; Beitz, 1999, pp. 149–53; Pogge, 1989, pp. 246–59). This global egalitarianism also seems to fit well with some of the basic intuitions that Rawls appeals to in developing his theory of social justice. Rawls appeals to the intuition that it is wrong for individuals' life-prospects to be radically worse than those of others because they are born into one class rather than another. We have seen that he builds on this intuition, arguing that it is no less objectionable for one person's prospects to be radically worse than another's due to poor endowments of talent (chapter 3). But isn't one's nationality similarly an arbitrary accident of birth like one's social class and natural ability? If so, why should we think it legitimate in principle for this specific accident of birth to give rise to inequalities in life-prospects (Beitz, 1983, 1999; Pogge, 1989; Caney, 2001a, 2001b, 2003)?[1]

2. *The internal challenge.* A second response to Rawls's theory of international justice takes the basic framework of the OPP as a given, but argues that representatives in the OPP will choose more egalitarian principles than Rawls suggests.[2] One focus of criticism is Rawls's assumption that peoples' representatives in the OPP care only that their societies have sufficient resources to establish and maintain just domestic institutions. While this is clearly something that should be of concern to representatives in the OPP, it is not clear why the capacity to establish and maintain just domestic institutions should exhaust the concern they have for their peoples' economic prospects. Why not assume that each OPP representative is interested more broadly in her people's economic well-being? Then the representatives may well support principles that go beyond the 'duty of assistance' that Rawls proposes (Pogge, 1994, pp. 208–11; Beitz, 2000, pp. 692–3; Caney, 2001a, p. 985). If Rawls's arguments concerning the domestic original position are accepted, then it looks as if they will agree to some analogue of the difference principle, perhaps that: economic inequality between peoples should be arranged so as to maximize the economic prospects of the worst-off group of peoples. (This is not quite the same as the global difference principle sketched above, as it focuses on peoples rather than individuals as the units of distributive concern. But the two principles might have similar implications in practice.)

Second, even if we grant Rawls the assumption that peoples' representatives in the OPP are concerned only to ensure that their peoples have sufficient resources to sustain a just domestic order, this concern itself gives the representatives reasons to want to limit economic inequality between peoples. This is because economic inequalities between peoples will translate into inequalities of power, and these could undermine the capacity of poorer peoples to protect their just domestic institutions from external pressures

(Pogge, 1994, pp. 213–14; see also Beitz, 2000, pp. 693–4; Caney, 2001a, p. 985).

How might one reply to these arguments for more egalitarian international economic arrangements than those implied by Rawls's proposed duty of assistance? So far as the radical challenge is concerned, the critic might return us to the question we briefly posed in chapter 1: What feature or features must a collection of individuals have in order for us to say that the value of equality applies straightforwardly to the distribution of goods within them? The radical challenge supposes that shared humanity and scarcity as such are the relevant features: whenever there are two or more people and scarce goods the distribution of goods between them stands in need of justification and this justification must give full weight to the egalitarian considerations we have canvassed in chapters 3 to 6. But there are alternative views of what makes a group a *community of equality* in this sense. For example, there is the view we outlined in chapter 1, according to which this justificatory demand applies only amongst individuals who share a duty of obedience and support to a common political authority (Nagel, 2005; see also Blake, 2002). Others might claim that this justificatory demand applies only to people who are engaged actively in economic cooperation with each other – people who, in Rawls's terminology, participate in a shared system of cooperation. If either of these views is correct, then we can reject the radical challenge to Rawls on the grounds that it is based fundamentally on a flawed view of what the community of equality is.

However, as a defence of Rawls's proposed duty of assistance against a more egalitarian account of international justice, this does not seem very promising. First, if it defends Rawls's position at all, it obviously defends it only against the radical challenge and not against the internal challenge. Second, even if we grant that common political authority or common participation in economic cooperation is what triggers the demand for equality-based justification, rather than the mere existence of human beings and scarce goods as such, this arguably offers only limited traction against the global egalitarian position. For it can be argued that these features – common political authority, common participation in economic cooperation – in fact already obtain to some extent at the global level. There is, clearly, very considerable economic cooperation between people of different countries which has major effects on individuals' life-prospects (the insight behind Charles Beitz's proposal for a global difference principle in Beitz, 1999; see also Pogge, 1989). Related to this, there is an emerging system of global economic governance which lays down binding rules that apply to individuals across countries. Although this does not amount to a 'world state', it represents a significant form of political authority in addition to that of the nation-state (Cohen and Sabel, 2006; Julius, 2006). In view of these developments, one might argue that the demand for equality-based justification is triggered when considering distributional issues across states; or that, even if the level of economic or governmental integration is not so great as to trigger this demand in full, it is sufficient to trigger more egalitarian principles of cross-national obligation than those we associate with a basic humanitarian minimum (Cohen and Sabel, 2006; Julius, 2006).

The strongest objection to global egalitarianism appeals to the need to accommodate *reasonable difference in shared ways of life* (for similar comment, see Beitz, 2000, p. 695). By reasonable difference here I mean two things. First, intelligent and well-intentioned people will disagree to some extent, and quite reasonably, about justice itself. The debates reviewed in this book are evidence in themselves of the potential for reasonable disagreement about the nature of justice. Second, within the bounds of reasonable disagreement about justice, groups of people might disagree about the importance of other values to pursue in common. The importance of economic growth itself could be one thing on which groups disagree. Surely any just global order must be structured in a way that accommodates these kinds of reasonable disagreement. Now the obvious way to accommodate these is to allow such groups some degree of political independence (for a related argument concerning justice within nations, see King, 2005). Within the bounds of their own political units, they can then establish institutions which reflect their values. However once groups start to pursue their distinctive values within their respective political units, some degree of economic inequality between them is likely to result.

For instance, if group A values economic growth more than group B, and this is reflected in the institutions of their societies, then in time group A might well end up richer than group B. Should the global order be structured so as to eliminate or prevent this inequality? Should it require group A to transfer some of its wealth to B so that the inequality between them is cancelled out? Describing a couple of cases like this, Rawls argues that the policy of enforced transfer is 'unacceptable' (Rawls, 1999b, pp. 117–18). In support of his claim one can argue that the egalitarian policy compromises the freedom of distinct groups to enjoy a common life based on their own values. Group A makes one choice about the importance of economic growth, and group B another, but under the proposed egalitarian scheme neither can really live with the consequences of its choice. This seems to degrade the choice that, out of respect for reasonable difference, we think they ought to have. Another way of expressing the point is to say that there is a conflict between global egalitarianism and the value of 'national self-determination' or local democracy (Miller, 2000b, pp. 161–79; Bertram, 2005).

What are we to make of this argument against global egalitarianism? One way to assess its significance is to return to the standpoint of the OPGI. In the OPGI we imagine individuals, ignorant of their own likely national position, choosing principles to regulate the global order. The foregoing argument shows that the parties in the OPGI will have one strong reason to choose principles that allow for the formation of politically independent groups and for the emergence of some economic inequality between them. But within the OPGI the parties will balance this consideration against other concerns that they have. They will not want a very high level of economic inequality between independent political units because, to repeat a point we made above, this in itself threatens the independence of poorer units (Pogge, 1994, pp. 213–14). In addition, one can argue that if the rationale for allowing some inequality is respect for reasonable difference in freely chosen collective ways of life then it is surely essential that people as individuals really do have the freedom to choose between the different ways of life that generate this inequality. The parties in the OPGI will want to ensure that if people do live in a poorer society, then this represents a genuinely free choice for them as individuals, based on distinctive values that they freely endorse. But for this to be a genuinely free choice, then arguably there must be decent opportunities to emigrate to richer communities. Thus, the parties in the OPGI might well insist that any economic inequalities that emerge between independent political units should be qualified by strong rights of emigration/immigration.[3]

In conclusion, Rawls's contention that international distributive concerns are exhausted by a limited duty of assistance seems highly implausible. Whether one adopts the radical standpoint of the OPGI or Rawls's own approach, based on what peoples' representatives would agree to in an OPP, there is good reason to think that a just international order will aim to moderate economic inequality between nations (over and above whatever equalization is implied by the duty of assistance).

A final thought: as we shall see shortly, some policies that arguably promote international egalitarian goals might make it harder for governments in richer nations to achieve domestic egalitarian goals. Another issue for consideration, therefore, is how to weigh the claims of global and domestic equality against each other should they conflict. We do not have space to consider the issue properly here. But, given the extreme character of global inequality in our world today, it does not seem very plausible to insist that rich countries should give full or even strong priority to domestic over global equality when the two conflict.

7.2   The pessimist's case

If today we have a growing appreciation that the demand for equality is in some significant (if still highly contested) sense a demand with global scope, many commentators are very pessimistic about the capacity of nation-states to meet equality's demands domestically, let alone on the international plane. This section sets out the pessimist's case. The following section concludes the book with a statement of the contrary position.

Take the case of Britain. In the period after the Second World War up to the 1970s, income inequality in Britain was quite stable. The Gini coefficient, which economists standardly use as a measure of inequality, bobbed up and down around 0.25 (Brewer et al., 2004).[4] However, in the 1980s, Britain experienced a rapid growth in income inequality; the Gini coefficient climbed to about 0.33, a very substantial increase which undid much of the earlier progress towards greater income equality in the post-war years. This upward trend is not peculiar to Britain, moreover. Table 7.1 shows the percentage change in the Gini coefficient for a range of countries in recent years; in virtually all cases, the Gini has increased.

In assessing trends in economic inequality, moreover, it is important to look at wealth not just income. Wealth inequality in Britain, as in all other countries, has always tended to be greater than income inequality. However, it declined over the post-war period up to the 1970s, and was then stable during the 1980s and for the first half of the 1990s, the Gini coefficient hovering at around 0.65. However, wealth inequality increased in the late 1990s, the Gini coefficient

Table 7.1   Percentage change in Gini coefficient
(disposable income, whole population)

Belgium (1985/96)	+10
France (1984/94)	0
Germany (West) (1984/94)	+7
Italy (1986/95)	+17
Netherlands (1987/94)	−5
Denmark (1987/97)	+1
Finland (1987/95)	+4
Norway (1986/95)	+7
Sweden (1987/95)	+12
United Kingdom (1986/95)	+28
United States (1986/95)	+24

Source: Esping-Anderson, 2005, in Giddens and Diamond (eds), 2005, p. 12.

rising to 0.68 in 1996 and 0.7 in 2002. To put this abstract figure in perspective: in 1991, the richest 10 per cent held 47 per cent of the nation's marketable wealth; by 2002, they owned 56 per cent. The poorest 50 per cent owned just 6 per cent of the nation's wealth in this year (Inland Revenue, 2004, table 13.5; figures for 2002 provisional).

What about equality of opportunity? As we noted in chapter 3, one indication of equality of opportunity is a society's level of social mobility. Recent research shows that the correlation between children's and parental incomes is actually greater for younger people in Britain than for older people, evidence that in one sense social mobility has declined in recent years, though other researchers argue that class mobility, as defined in chapter 3, has remained unchanged (Blanden et al., 2004).[5]

It might be argued that these trends simply make it more urgent that the government act to promote equality. However, the pessimist argues, this misses the point that it is getting ever harder for governments to do so. There are a number of reasons for this.

The first is *economic globalization*. This refers to growth of trade and in the mobility of capital and labour about the world. As a result of these developments, governments are more constrained in how much they can tax and spend to promote greater equality than they were in the more closed economies of the 1950s–60s. If they raise taxes and spending too much, they will prompt a flight of capital from their country. This will damage economic growth, and make them very unpopular with the electorate. Note that this is perhaps one area in which there is possibly a tension between international and domestic egalitarianism. The impact of globalization on poorer nations is a complex and uneven one (Held, 2004, pp. 34–54). But to the extent that it does improve prospects for poorer nations, then there is an international egalitarian case for it, although this will make it harder for governments in the richer nations to reduce inequality domestically.

A second important factor is the *change in the class structure* of advanced economies brought about by the decline of manufacturing and the growth of service-sector employment (Crouch, 2004; see also Hobsbawm, 1981). In the industrial economies of the mid-twentieth century, industrial workers –

Marx's proletariat – had a relatively clear class identity linked to political support for parties of the left that stood for economic equality. High levels of unionization helped to maintain this identity. To maintain electoral popularity, all governments, even those of the right, were forced to adopt some measures of social welfare and redistribution. However, in place of the old industrial working class, there is now a large group of service-sector workers who do not have the same sense of class membership and political identity. Consequently, parties of the left, who notionally support economic equality, now lack a strong social base.

Third, there is the problem of *decline in civic engagement*. The mass publics of democracies such as Britain and the United States are less engaged with civic and political life than in the past (Putnam, 2000). The causes of this are multiple, but include: pressures of working life; generational differences in values; and the impact of electronic entertainment (notably television) on how people enjoy their leisure (Putnam, 2000, pp. 277–84). This decline in civic engagement has led, in turn, to an erosion of what sociologists call 'social capital': the reservoir of trust and respect between people which facilitates social cooperation. Empirical studies show that there is a correlation between lower social capital and higher inequality (Putnam, 2000, pp. 358–60). One explanation for this is that as social capital declines, and people become less trustful towards one another, support for redistributive taxation and social spending, which tend to reduce economic inequality, declines.[6] Thus, if the decline in civic engagement continues, we can expect it to become more difficult to sustain equality-promoting policies.

Fourth, a related problem is posed by *increasing cultural and ethnic diversity*. Redistribution, for the sake of greater equality, requires that citizens trust one another. When a society is reasonably homogeneous in terms of its culture and ethnicity, the basis for trust is there. But as society becomes multiethnic and multicultural, the basis for trust is weakened. It thus becomes harder to sustain support for equality-promoting, redistributive politics. This may be one reason why an ethnically and culturally pluralist society like the United States does not have levels of income redistribution comparable to more homogeneous European societies (Alesina et al., 2001; Alesina and Glaeser, 2004). Here again there might well be a painful trade-off between the demands of international and domestic egalitarianism. International egalitarianism arguably calls for relaxed immigration policies on the part of nations with advanced economies. But relaxed immigration policies might well make these societies more multicultural and multiethnic and so weaken their ability to achieve domestic equality.

A fifth and crucial factor is *the lack of a credible alternative to free-market capitalism*. For much of the nineteenth and twentieth centuries, hopes for economic egalitarianism were closely intertwined with the expectation that it is possible to construct a wholly different, alternative economic system to capitalism. But the experience of Soviet Communism has taught us that there is essentially no such alternative. We are, as one commentator has infamously put it, at 'the end of history', in which capitalism, embedded in a system of electoral democracy, has triumphed over rival social systems (Fukuyama, 1992).

Capitalism is here to stay because we cannot conceive of any reasonable alternative; and in its contemporary globalized and post-industrial form, capitalism does not provide a very favourable terrain on which to promote economic equality.

7.3   The optimist's case

In making any assessment of the prospects of equality politics, it is vital to take a long-term view. If we look back to 1789, the year of the French Revolution, and ask what kind of progress we have made in relation to equality, we will see just how much has been accomplished (see also Wilkinson, 2005, p. 248). Focusing on Britain, what do we see? We see movement towards political equality. Whereas only a minority of men had the vote in Britain in 1789, now virtually all adults do. The status of women in society has radically changed. Women have claimed equality with men, and have achieved real gains in this respect in areas such as the vote, political office, employment, education, marital law and social welfare. Wealth inequality remains high. But it is still considerably less unequal than it was at the start of the nineteenth, or even at the start of the twentieth, century. While income inequality remains high, and has risen in more recent years, the significance of such inequality is diminished by the various 'social rights' that government continues to provide (Marshall, 1950). These include the right to primary and secondary education and the right to health care under the National Health Service, which is based on the principle that people should receive health care on the basis of need rather than ability to pay. So while there may have been setbacks to the cause of equality in recent years, the long-term picture is one of progress on a number of fronts. If in the Britain of the 1790s one had painted a picture of a society as egalitarian as Britain is today, most people would have regarded you as a fool. ('What? *Women* to have the vote? Everyone to have a right to education and health care *at the government's expense?* You must be living in a dreamworld!') But these changes have happened, despite many periods of setback along the way. So who is to say what the Britain (if there is a Britain) of 2210 might not look like?

The pessimist points to five factors that will work against equality politics in the future. But is the picture really as gloomy as she thinks?

The pessimist claims first that economic globalization severely constrains the capacity of national governments to promote equality. Even if this is true, however, we need not conclude that equality must be abandoned as a political goal. Perhaps we should try to limit or even reverse economic globalization so as to give some power back to national governments (Woodin and Lucas, 2004), though careful consideration would need to be given to the impact this could have on international egalitarianism. Or perhaps we should build supranational institutions that can pursue equality more effectively in a globalized economy (Van Parijs, 1995, pp. 226–30; Held, 2004, pp. 73–116). Moreover, is globalization as significant as the pessimist claims? As a matter of fact, tax burdens have not fallen in many advanced economies since the 1980s (Held, 2004, table 2, p. 32). The mobility of capital does mean that if a government adopts policies that look likely to provoke distributional conflict and inflationary pressures, then there will be rapid capital flight, pressurizing the government to stop. But if the government manages to build a consensus around its distributional goals, that extends to the various groups of workers and employers and other affected interests, then its policies will not provoke distributional conflict and so should not provoke capital flight. The challenge remains what it has always been: to build broad popular support for egalitarian policies (Glyn, 1997/98, 2006, pp. 156–83).

However, is it realistic to think that egalitarians can build such support? Recall the pessimist's second claim, that changes in the class structure of advanced economies, in particular the decline of the industrial working class, have deprived egalitarian politics of a solid social base. This is certainly an important development. Marx argued that capitalism would simplify class division, splitting society into a large majority camp of impoverished proletarians and a small group of property owners (Marx, 2002 [1848]). As a matter of rationality, the proletariat would seek to throw off its chains and, given its numerical strength, would inevitably succeed in the end. This picture no longer looks credible. At least within the advanced capitalist countries, the class structure has become much more complex than Marx predicted. History clearly is not a train, driven by the industrial working class, racing with red flags flying, towards a destination called equality. All that said, however, we certainly have not entered a world in which workers no longer have grievances. Many of the new service-sector workers are crowded into low-skilled, poorly paid and often somewhat demeaning jobs that offer little prospect of upward mobility; and even many of the more educated, better-paid service sector workers face pressing problems to do with perceived job insecurity, pension insecurity, work intensification and poor work–life balance (Crouch, 2004, pp. 66–7). The task for egalitarian politics is to persuade workers in both groups that these problems are best addressed through political programmes that rest on an ethic of solidarity, rather than through individual effort alone.

At this mention of 'solidarity', however, our pessimist might now remind us of her third and fourth points: the decline in civic engagement and the growth of cultural and ethnic diversity. The decline in civic engagement perhaps implies something akin to what Tocqueville termed individualism: 'a mature and calm feeling, which disposes each member of the community to sever himself from the mass of his fellows and to draw apart with his family and friends, so that after he has thus formed a little circle of his own, he willingly leaves society at large to itself' (Tocqueville, 1990 [1840], p. 98). The growth in diversity allegedly generates distrust between members of different ethnic groups. Both developments thus work against the ethic of solidarity that a politics of equality needs. However, neither point is as conclusive as it might seem. First, as regards diversity, the evidence linking greater diversity to distrust and weakened support for the welfare state is in fact mixed and strongly contested (Pearce, 2004; Banting, 2005; Taylor-Gooby, 2005). Critics argue that the impact of diversity on the willingness of publics to support social spending is strongly influenced by different national institutions and circumstances. Hence, even if diversity has substantially weakened support for social spending in the United States, we should not assume that as other countries become more diverse their levels of social spending, or of economic inequality, will move in the direction of the United States. The importance of national institutions brings us to a second, related point. As regards both developments, it is a mistake to assume that there is nothing government can do either to combat them (civic engagement) or to mitigate their potentially divisive effects (diversity). Both developments raise important questions about the design of the public sphere; that is, about the way in which institutions work (or don't work) to cultivate a sense of shared identity and purpose amongst people as citizens (Pearce, 2004). The challenge to egalitarians is to look at existing political and civic institutions and ask: How could these be redesigned to strengthen a sense of common citizenship? Do civic education modules in schools have a role? National service programmes like those mentioned in chapter 3? Or proposals for creating a more participatory form of democracy of the kind we sketched in chapter 2? There is an important research agenda here for the political sociologist, which might yield interesting and helpful results.

Moreover, the point that rising inequality seems to be related to a decline in social capital, symptomatic of a worsening in the quality of social relationships, is one that the egalitarian can use to build popular support for equality-promoting policies. A large body of research points to a strong association between high economic inequality on the one hand and high levels of distrust, crime and lower average levels of health on the other (Wilkinson, 2005). Against this background, the egalitarian can say: 'Look, do you want to live in a society where people trust one another, respect each other and do not have high levels of stress? If so, then you should support efforts to make our society more economically equal because research shows that it is very hard to sustain trust and respect and to avoid high levels of stress in highly unequal societies.'[7]

Now the pessimist might turn to her final point: even if equality is desirable and we could build popular support for it, there is simply no way we can achieve it in a modern market economy. There is no credible alternative today to free-market capitalism, an economic system that necessarily generates high levels of economic inequality.

Of all the pessimist's points, however, this is perhaps the least convincing. It is true that the classical model of socialism as an economic system that simply *negates* capitalism, replacing private property with state property, and the market with the centralized planning of production, is discredited (Miller, 1989b; Roemer, 1994). Such an economic system seems unable to provide for freedom, or efficiency, or, indeed, political, social and economic equality. However, state socialism and free-market capitalism do not exhaust the possibilities. There is a huge variation in the kind of capitalist societies in the world, ranging from ones which come close to the ideal of 'laissez-faire' to ones that embed the market in expansive welfare states (Hall and Soskice, 2001). Levels of economic inequality also vary quite considerably across these societies (Kenworthy, 2004). Over the course of the past century, economists sympathetic to equality have given a lot of thought as to how we can achieve greater equality within a market economy, and this has now produced a rich, suggestive literature. Market socialists have argued that it is possible for productive assets to be owned publicly or cooperatively while the market works to guide resource allocation (Miller, 1989b; Estrin and Le Grand, 1989). Others have argued for the retention of private property in productive assets but for policies that will serve to distribute these assets, or an equivalent income stream, much more equally than at present (Van Parijs, 1995; Ackerman and Alstott, 1999). A number of writers have put forward proposals that combine elements of these two models. Notable examples include James Meade's work on a 'property-owning democracy' or 'partnership economy' (Meade, 1964, 1989); and Robin Blackburn's proposals for a 'complex socialism' based on popularly owned and controlled pension funds (Blackburn, 1999, 2002, forthcoming).[8] It is simply not true that we lack plausible models of alternatives to free-market capitalism, and the real-world diversity of capitalism itself should make us wary of assuming that there is only one way to organize economic activity, one that is profoundly at odds with equality.

The pessimist's case is overstated. She has identified some major obstacles to the politics of equality. But she goes too far in asserting that these cannot be overcome. The truth is that there have always been major obstacles in the way of progress to equality. At times in the past it has looked as if equality gains from an earlier period would be lost and that the whole modern movement towards equality would be decisively reversed. Such was the case, for example, in the 1930s. Many then argued that the economic problems of democratic states like Britain, France and the United States pointed to the redundancy of democracy (see, for example, Wells, 1928). The rise to power of fascists in many European countries (along with Soviet Communism) seemed to confirm this analysis (Burnham, 1941). Of course, it was only after enormous struggle and sacrifice that fascism was defeated. But it *was* defeated. The writers who so confidently predicted the demise of democracy were wrong.

The key points are these: first, that the demand for equality, in all its complexity, retains its moral force; and, second, that energetic efforts to promote equality in the past have overcome major obstacles, no less considerable than those we face today. If the demand for equality does have this moral force, and, despite the obstacles in our way, there is at least the possibility of making our social world more equal, how can we choose not to do our bit to bring this about?

Notes

Chapter 1   The Demand for Equality

1   Clayton and Williams, 2000, provide an excellent discussion of the topic of why and how we might value equality, to which I am indebted both here and in chapter 5, section 5.2.

2   Williams points out that racists are often too embarrassed simply to assert that one ethnic group is worthy of less respect than another because of the colour of its skin. Racists try to offer a rationale for discrimination by arguing that an apparently arbitrary characteristic such as skin colour is correlated with other characteristics, such as moral corruption, that supposedly make the proposed discrimination non-arbitrary. 'The Nazi "anthropologists" who tried to construct theories of Aryanism,' writes Williams, 'were paying, in very poor coin, the homage of irrationality to reason' (Williams, 1973, p. 233). Similar remarks apply, I think, to efforts to rationalize unequal treatment based on gender, social class or sexual orientation.

3   The importance of thinking about the 'social bases of self-respect' is identified by Jean-Jacques Rousseau in his *Discourse on Inequality* (1984 [1755]). In this highly influential essay, Rousseau depicts modern society as a competitive scramble for esteem (*amour propre*). People derive their sense of self-worth from being seen as superior to others. If such sentiments are built into our human nature, then the prospects for an egalitarian society look dim. Our innate desire to establish ourselves as socially superior to others, to be esteemed above them as rich and powerful, will undermine egalitarian institutions.

However, recent commentators have emphasized that, in Rousseau's view, the basic need to have one's worth affirmed by society need not be satisfied only in this way. We can also derive our sense of self-worth from arrangements which affirm our value as equals to others (J. Cohen, 1997b, forthcoming; Bertram, 2004, pp. 17–38; Dent, 1988, 2005, pp. 68–72, 104–6). In this case, my sense of self-worth consists in the sense that I am, fundamentally, just as much a citizen as you, no more no less, entitled to the same say in public matters and the same consideration in making laws. However, if social institutions allow substantial inequalities in politics and the economy, then it may become difficult for us to sustain this egalitarian sense of self-worth. Then we may get drawn into the kind of competitive scramble that Rousseau depicts and laments. It is probably fair to say that as a political project, egalitarianism is feasible in the long term only if these hypotheses about human psychology are broadly correct. For a comprehensive and instructive overview of relevant zoological and anthropological literatures, which seems broadly supportive of Rousseau's view, see Wilkinson, 2005, pp. 235–82. In Wilkinson's words (pp. 264–5): 'We must never lose sight of the fact that we have built-in equipment both for the highly social strategies of interaction associated with equality and for the antisocial strategies of dominance behaviour. . . . More unequal social environments increase concern for social status and lead to emphasis on dominance behaviour . . . contrasting sharply with the more inclusive and affiliative strategies associated with greater equality.'

4   For example, returning to Baldwin's argument, evidence suggests that status inequality between blacks and whites in the United States contributes to health inequality between the racial groups. Blacks have poorer health than whites on average in part because blacks on average have lower incomes and poorer jobs. But blacks also enjoy poorer health on average than whites with similar income and jobs. Statistically, race seems to exert an independent, negative impact on health across all levels of income and occupational class. Part of the explanation is that the lower status of blacks generates stress and reduces self-esteem which, in turn, damage health. See Barry, 2005, pp. 77–82; and Wilkinson, 2005, pp. 14–15, 76, 228–9; Wilkinson's book provides an excellent comprehensive overview of research on the relationship between status inequality and health.

5   But note that the supporter of the priority view will have to bring in some further principle to break the tie between X and Y.

Chapter 2 Democracy

1 Plato usually speaks through the figure of Socrates in his dialogues and this raises the question of whether Plato is presenting Socrates' views or whether he is presenting his own views through the voice of a fictional Socrates. There is no clear answer to this question, but most experts agree that in earlier dialogues, such as the *Protagoras, Gorgias* and *The Apology*, we are hearing something close to Socrates' own views, whereas in a later dialogue like the *Republic* the Socrates character is a mouthpiece for Plato's own views, which represent a particular line of development from Socrates' views.

2 If all candidates are ignoring the interests of the poorer classes in an election for office, then each candidate has an obvious incentive to break with the rest and appeal to the poorer classes so as to win their votes.

3 Another important feature of Aristotle's theory of the good polity is his advice that the lawmaker seek to create a large middle class of middling property owners to stand between the rich and the poor and temper their excesses. See Aristotle, 1948, book 4, chapters 11–13. We should note that Plato also discusses a mixed constitution in *The Laws*. See Plato, 2004, pp. 98–111. Nelson, 2004, chapter 1, provides a helpful overview of the relationship between Plato, Aristotle and Polybius.

4 Clearly, there is an important difference here as between those who insist on *actual consent* as a condition of political legitimacy and those who merely require *hypothetical consent*. I shall not explore this important distinction here, but for helpful discussion, see Waldron, 1993a.

5 Hobbes does not rule out political equality altogether. But he states and defends a clear preference for monarchy. See Hobbes, 1985 [1651], chapter 19.

6 Indeed some commentators have argued that a close reading of Locke's text indicates that he supported a political system in which authority is wholly in the hands of the propertied classes. However, while I suspect this was Locke's preference, I do not think the text of the *Second Treatise* clearly points to a system of this type. Contextual political reasons may have led Locke to be purposefully ambiguous as to his preferences. For further discussion, see MacPherson, 1962, chapter 5; Ryan, 1965; and Ashcraft, 1986.

7 There has been much debate over whether the Levellers were or were not committed to universal male suffrage. For a compelling contribution to the debate, see Hampsher-Monk, 1976, who argues that the basic Leveller position was one of support for universal male suffrage but that the Levellers were prepared

to press less radical demands at certain junctures as a compromise with more conservative groups.

8   Rainborough was also clearly worried that the rich would use a monopoly of political authority to trample on the interests of the poor; see Sharp (ed.), 1998, p. 109.

9   This point is crucial to understanding what Rousseau means when he says that laws are to express the 'general will'. The general will is not simply the aggregate will of the citizen assembly, but a will that is oriented to the good of the citizenry as a whole. It is general both in terms of the constituency it issues from and in terms of the interests it consciously serves.

10 For discussion of the variant of the respect argument presented in Rawls's work, see J. Cohen, 2003, specifically pp. 108–11.

11 In emphasizing the value of public participation in democratic government, Tocqueville perhaps had his sight immediately on the problem of 'individualism' (which we will briefly elaborate in chapter 7) rather than that of majority tyranny. However, the two problems are closely related in that the erosion of a sense of public responsibility associated with individualism is likely to heighten the risk of majority tyranny.

12 As a matter of fact, many would argue that the Supreme Court played a key role in expanding protection for individual rights in the period of the 1950s–1970s and particularly in securing the civil rights of African-Americans. But its record historically is a distinctly mixed one.

13 There is a sense in which this applies even in the United States. If a large majority of the people are very keen on a certain law and the Supreme Court declares it unconstitutional, there is always the possibility that the people who want the law can muster support for a constitutional amendment, though the process of amendment can be a very demanding and time-consuming one.

14 See also Cohen and Rogers, 1995b, p. 256; Cohen and Sabel, 1997, p. 320. Duncan and Lukes, 1963, also provide an excellent response to scepticism concerning participatory democracy in Anglo-American post-war political thought.

15 The basic idea is that national legislatures establish basic goals in these areas, but that responsibility on how to reach them is then devolved to local bodies. Each local body would be in a network with other local bodies, to facilitate mutual learning, and would be monitored (and possibly sanctioned for poor performance) from the centre.

16 Citizens' juries are small groups chosen to deliberate on a specific question or issue and to offer advisory prescriptions based on informed discussion. Deliberative opinion polls focus on larger sets of people who are asked their views on a subject

following a period of discussion with experts and debate amongst themselves.

17   See also Fishkin, 1995; Dryzek, 2000. There are important differences between these thinkers, as well as a common emphasis on the value of shared, public, morally informed discussion. For a helpful overview, see Freeman, 2000.

Chapter 3   Meritocracy

1   Usually such legislation will carry an exemption for exceptional cases in which one or more of these characteristics is reasonably seen as relevant to someone's ability to do a given job. For example, it seems reasonable to insist that those running shelters for women escaping domestic abuse be women, and that those employed as priests, rabbis or ministers have the religion of their respective faith groups.

2   It might be argued that if customers prefer white waiters and waitresses, then race is relevant to their suitability for the job and so it is not in fact genuine discrimination for employers to choose white job applicants over black applicants. However, if the consumers' preferences just reflect racial prejudice, then it remains the case that blacks are being denied equal access to certain positions for no reason other than their colour and nothing to do with their competence in waitering or waitressing as such. For this reason, most meritocrats would argue that we should not allow the consumers' preferences to enter at all into an evaluation of the 'merit' of black job candidates as compared with white. See Miller, 2000a, p. 169.

3   This is an example of how strict application of the merit principle is not always efficient. Certainly for the employer the costs of applying it outweigh the benefits. If this is also true for society as a whole then the anti-discrimination laws impose a net cost on society. Thus, the argument for applying the merit principle must rest on its link to desert.

4   What Crosland refers to here as 'nepotism' and 'class favouritism' arguably represent forms of discrimination, and so would be opposed by the weak, as well as strong, meritocrat. The inequalities in educational opportunity and in 'inherited property' that he refers to are more exclusively the concern of the strong meritocrat.

5   Note that it is much less obvious what equality of opportunity in education amounts to for children who have unequal potentials. Should resources be used to develop the abilities of high-potential students as much as possible or to bring low potential

students up as much they can? For a helpful discussion which clarifies the issues, see Brighouse, 2002, pp. 17–20.

6 There are in fact two approaches to the study of social mobility (Bowles, Gintis and Osborne Groves, 2005, pp. 1–3). The approach discussed in the main text, favoured by sociologists, focuses on movement between distinct groups or classes. Another approach, favoured by economists, focuses on the relationship between the incomes, earnings or wealth of parents and those of their offspring. I shall make some reference to studies of this second kind in the course of the discussion.

7 For an alternative class schema, drawing on Marxist social theory, see Erik Olin Wright, 1997.

8 Sociologists distinguish between *absolute* and *relative* social mobility. Absolute mobility concerns the proportion of people from a given social class entering another class. We have seen that absolute mobility out of the working class is quite high among sons born in 1958. Relative mobility concerns the chances of people born into one class ending up in a given class position compared to those born into another class. We have seen that relative mobility rates between salariat and working-class sons born in 1958 are very unequal (with respect to ending up in these social classes). While a good many sons of working-class families born in 1958 have moved up the social ladder, statistically speaking, compared with the sons of the salariat, they still had a less than equal chance of ending up in a high place on the ladder. As the economy grew, the share of working-class jobs in overall employment fell and the share of middle-class jobs rose, and, in order to fuel the expansion in the middle class, a large number of working-class children were drawn into middle-class jobs. But the chance of getting jobs in the higher social classes were still much better for those sons born to fathers in higher-class positions.

9 For a more general critique of the use of IQ measures in discussions of meritocracy, see Barry, 2005, pp. 109–27. Barry points out that the whole idea of a fixed natural or innate ability level is a potentially misleading simplification (Barry, 2005, pp. 122–4). Imagine we have two children, Greg and Helen. Their genetic endowments are such that if they are both raised in similarly poor environments, Helen will emerge as the apparently most intelligent or talented one. But if they are both raised in similarly good environments, Greg will emerge as the most intelligent or otherwise talented. So which one has the higher innate ability?

10 For example, imagine that a certain proportion of people born into all social classes have a strong innate desire to live as adults

amongst the kind of people they grew up with. In the case of children born into higher social classes, this desire will make them aspire to stay in this class and to get the necessary qualifications. In the case of children born into lower social classes, however, this desire will tend to dampen down aspirations for higher-class jobs and to get the necessary qualifications. In this case, motivational differences will help explain why individuals' class of origin is statistically related to their class of destination. But it is not clear that we should interpret this specific sort of motivational difference as inequality of opportunity. Or, if it is a kind of inequality of opportunity, it is not clear that we should regard it as morally objectionable.

11   Indeed, as we shall see in chapter 7, in the British case there is some evidence that class inheritance has increased in recent years.

12   The term has, however, shifted slightly in its meaning since Young wrote. Young speaks of 'the meritocracy' meaning the *class* of people who come out on top under conditions of real equality of opportunity, whereas these days the term is more usually used, as I have used it here, to refer to a *social system* which exhibits equality of opportunity.

13   To be clear, the suggestion is not that employers should pay wages on this basis, but that society should use taxes and subsidies to achieve this goal.

Chapter 4   Luck Egalitarianism

1   Dworkin's hypothetical insurance market is not the only framework that has been proposed for thinking about just levels of transfer to the handicapped. One other proposal, intended to handle inequality in all internal resources, and originating with Bruce Ackerman, is that of *undominated diversity*. Starting from a position of equality in external resources, we ask if anyone has such a poor endowment of internal resources that everyone prefers to have their own bundle of internal and (equal) external resources to this person's bundle. If there is such a person, we then transfer extra external resources to them until at least one person regards this expanded bundle as preferable to their own. We do this for all those with poor endowments of internal resources. The main objection to the approach is that it seems to render the level of transfer to those with severe handicaps extremely vulnerable to people with idiosyncratic preferences. See Ackerman, 1980; Van Parijs, 1995, chapter 3.

2   That is, in the same way that people reasonably disagree about the importance of happiness to the good life, so they can and will reasonably disagree about the importance of success in achieving one's goals to the overall goodness or value of a life. One person might choose goals with a view to making sure they have a good prospect of success in achieving them, while another might think your choice of goals should be based much more on what you think has value independently of your prospects of actually achieving them. Going back to our earlier example, one person might decide to pursue a life of moderate scientific ambition in which there is a good chance of achieving her modest goals, while another might think it more worthwhile to raise her sights and to try to tackle a single big question even though the likelihood of success is low. See Dworkin, 2000, pp. 30–2.

3   For a stimulating critique of Dworkin's equality of resources from the standpoint of the capabilities approach, see Williams, 2002; and for a forceful reply, Dworkin, 2002.

4   In G. A. Cohen's words (Cohen, 1995b, p. 68): 'According to the thesis of self-ownership, each person possesses over himself, as a matter of moral right, all those rights that a slaveholder has over a complete chattel slave as a matter of legal right, and he is entitled, morally speaking, to dispose over himself in the way such a slaveholder is entitled, legally speaking, to dispose over his slave.'

5   Imagine a society in which there are two groups. There is a group of talented workers and a group of untalented workers. (Recall that by 'talented' and 'untalented' we mean talented in terms of earning income through the application of labour; people can of course be very talented or untalented in other respects, but these are not germane to our use of the terms here.) An egalitarian political theorist has given this world an economic constitution under which all talented workers are required to transfer 50 per cent of their labour incomes to a fund that will be used to subsidize the labour incomes of the untalented. Now, it also so happens that the talented are all devout Christians and the untalented are all militant atheists. As militant atheists, the untalented like to burn Bibles in joyful atheistical rituals and they are keen to use the funds they get from the taxes on the labour incomes of the talented to buy Bibles for this purpose. Thus, in this world, the tax-transfer scheme puts the talented in the following position: if they choose to work to create resources to advance their Christian conception of the good, then they have no choice also but to generate resources that will in fact be used by others, the

untalented, to attack and mock Christianity. The talented see their efforts harnessed for the benefit of others, and they then see the benefits of their efforts being turned against their own values. Morally speaking, is this a problem?

6   In his most recent book, Dworkin argues that his equality of resources theory recommends a system of support for the unemployed in which entitlement is linked with willingness-to-work and to retraining. This sounds a lot like what Anderson recommends. See Dworkin, 2000, pp. 331–40; Anderson, 1999, pp. 318, 323–5. Both would treat dependent care responsibilities as moderating a duty to work in the formal economy as a condition of basic income entitlement. It should be noted that some thinkers whom Anderson locates in the luck egalitarian camp advocate unconditional basic income entitlements. See, in particular, Van Parijs, 1995, for an attempt to justify an unconditional basic income, using a version of Dworkin's theory of the initial auction in which jobs are included as external resources in the auction. See also van Donselaar, 1997, for a challenging critique of Van Parijs's argument.

Chapter 5   Equality and Incentives

1   It is not altogether clear that Jay meant this because there is an ambiguity in the phrase 'society as a whole would be poorer'. Even if total output falls as we compress inequalities of reward, some groups in society could become better off. Low-paid groups could benefit more from increased equality than they suffer from the fall in total output that this more equal division causes. In such a case, there is a sense in which 'society as a whole' would *not* be poorer even though 'the whole output of goods and services is lower'.

2   Hobhouse clearly worked with very traditional assumptions about the division of paid and domestic labour within households. As we shall see in chapter 6 (section 6.1), these assumptions have long been called into question by the feminist movement.

3   What if two or more distributions give the worst-off group the same? Then, in Rawls's view, we should choose the one that is better for the next worst-off group, and so on all the way up to the best-off group. Thus if we had to choose between distribution A in which the worst off have 10 and the best off have 20, and distribution B in which the worst off have 10 and the best off have 30, and there are no other groups, Rawls

would have us choose B. However, if the alternative to A was distribution C in which the best off again get 30 but the worst off get slightly less at 9.5, Rawls would insist on A over C. See Rawls, 1999a, p. 72.

4 In response to the 'surfer objection' that I will discuss below, Rawls in his later work also adds 'leisure-time' to the list of goods in this index. See Rawls, 2001, p. 179; Van Parijs, 2003.

5 Rawls also factors in the concern that economic inequality might undermine political equality. His first principle of justice requires that economic arrangements be compatible with what he calls the 'fair value' of political freedoms. Significant economic inequality could undermine the fair value of these liberties for the less well off. See Rawls, 1993, pp. 324–31.

6 To be precise, the choice Rawls presents to the people in the original position is between justice as fairness as a whole, which includes the difference principle, and the average welfare principle.

7 A further very important argument of Rawls's appeals to the idea of 'stability'. A principle of justice is stable, in Rawls's sense, when its application tends to win the support and allegiance of those who have to live under it. Rawls argues that the average welfare principle is not stable in this sense. Some people may be compelled to lead very impoverished lives under the principle and they will reasonably feel hostility to the principle. In contrast, justice as fairness, which includes the difference principle, does not call upon anyone to sacrifice their basic well-being for the good of the community and so can elicit ongoing allegiance. See Rawls, 1999a, pp. 154–5.

8 Moreover, it has some empirical support. In psychological experiments designed to simulate decision-making in the original position, participants have tended to plump for a principle like this over both the difference principle and the average welfare principle. See Frolich and Oppenheimer, 1992.

9 Marx himself expected technological development to make it possible to reduce reliance on material incentives under communism. However, in the twentieth century Marxists took power in countries that were technologically quite undeveloped. This led them either to embrace the need for incentive-based inequalities of reward and/or to put a strong emphasis, like Hobhouse, on moral transformation, the creation of a new 'socialist man', to make it possible to sustain output without the need for sizeable monetary incentives. In the words of Ernesto Che Guevara: 'we struggle against the predominance of material incentives, for it would signify delaying the devel-

opment of socialist morality' (Che Guevara, 1997 [1964], p. 177). A focus on cooperative work ethos is also a key feature of R. H. Tawney's vision of a 'functional society' (Tawney, 1948 [1920]).

10   This alludes to what Cohen calls the 'interpersonal test'. 'This tests how robust a policy argument is, by subjecting it to variation with respect to who is speaking and/or who is listening when the argument is presented. The test asks whether the argument could serve as a justification for a mooted policy when uttered by any member of society to any other member' (Cohen, 1995a [1992], p. 348). Some arguments that seem persuasive when presented impersonally ('we should allow incentives so as to encourage the talented to work hard'), may seem much less persuasive when they are translated into interpersonal terms ('you unskilled people better let us talented have high incomes or we won't do any work').

11   Williams, 1998, also emphasizes the difficulty of making individual adherence to an appropriate work ethos a matter of public knowledge.

12   Joshua Cohen argues that certain background institutional features of a society satisfying Rawls's principles of justice – such as political equality – would themselves shape social norms in a way that would discourage objectionable incentives claims. See J. Cohen, 2001.

13   A further question arises when we probe the nature of the satisfaction that Carens envisages people will derive from meeting their duty to maximize pre-tax income. According to Carens, a key source of social-duty satisfaction will be the esteem that people get in return for fulfilling this duty. So, in effect, what he seems to be envisaging is a system in which esteem has the same place in people's hierarchy of values as income does in a conventional capitalist society, and in which people are rewarded with unequal esteem for unequal productive efforts, rather than with unequal income. But then in what way is the system he envisages really more egalitarian than the conventional capitalist alternative? To this Carens might reply that the *opportunity* to get esteem is much more equal in the market system he envisages than is the opportunity to acquire income in a conventional capitalist economy. In the conventional capitalist system, people with more talent have greater opportunity to acquire income. But in a Carensian market economy they will not have greater opportunity to get esteem than their less talented fellows, because esteem depends on how far one maximizes one's *capacity* to generate pre-tax income, and both talented and untalented workers can choose to maximize their

respective capacities to generate pre-tax income, and so obtain equal esteem.

Chapter 6   Equality and Difference

1   Women in full-time employment earn on average 82 per cent of what men in full-time employment earn (Charles, 2002, p. 29). This difference in earnings is compounded further by the fact that women are more likely to work part time: in 1994 78 per cent of all part-time jobs were held by women (Crompton, 1997, p. 32). While about 16 per cent of white women in jobs are in professional, managerial or employer jobs, the comparable figure for white men is 30 per cent (Charles, 2002, pp. 24–5, table 2.1, originally from Modood et al., 1997).

2   See also Tully, 1995; Parekh, 1997, 1999.

3   Arguments for multiculturalism sometimes appeal to the idea of reparations: culture-protecting group-specific rights are defended on the grounds that they represent an appropriate way of making reparation to a group that has suffered historical injustice. However, proponents of multiculturalism also appeal to the value of equality in a way that does not presuppose any reparative claim. I focus on this kind of argument in the main text. Note that where there is a valid reparative claim it requires further argument to show that it is most appropriately met through culture-protecting group-specific rights rather than, say, by cash transfers to members of the relevant groups.

4   However, Kymlicka does not think that a liberal state should necessarily enforce liberal norms on an illiberal cultural group living within its territory. See Kymlicka, 1995, pp. 94–5, 163–70.

5   Note that the alternative policy offers assistance and compensation for the costs involved in learning to function competently in the mainstream culture. It does not offer compensation to the minority group for the loss of its original culture as such.

6   *Department of Human Resources of Oregon v. Smith*, 494 US 872 (1990).

7   For somewhat conflicting views on the interests which properly constrain exemptionism, see Gutmann, 1995; and Galston, 2002, pp. 93–123. To some extent the disagreement between them turns on empirical questions about the impact that specific exemptions are likely to have; but it also reflects genuine moral disagreement about the weight we should give to values

such as equality of opportunity and the promotion of a capacity for active democratic citizenship as against the free exercise of religion.

8   Rawls returns to the status of the family in his theory of justice, responding to the criticism of Okin and others, in 'The Idea of Public Reason Revisited' in Rawls, 1999b, pp. 129–80, specifically pp. 156–64.

Chapter 7   The Future of Equality

1   Pursuing this thought, Simon Caney argues for a principle of 'global fair equality of opportunity' which holds that 'people of the same ability and same drive should have equal opportunity to positions of the same standard of living'; and for global application of the principle of 'equal remuneration for equal work' (Caney, 2003, p. 299). As Caney puts it: 'Would it not be a violation of natural justice to say, "Well, you've done the same amount of work as John Smith and produced something of equal worth but because you're Iranian you should get less"?' See also Fabre, 2003, for a radical cosmopolitan view.

2   Some critics are proponents of versions of both the radical and the internal challenges. Thomas Pogge, for example, outlines a version of the radical challenge in Pogge, 1989, and a version of the internal challenge in Pogge, 1994.

3   Thinking back to the issues discussed in chapter 6, note that this rationale for allowing high levels of immigration is not consistent with a claim that immigrant groups be supported in maintaining their culture of origin. For the rationale is that the immigrants endorse the values of the host nation and wish to share in the common way of life that expresses these values.

4   The Gini coefficient ranges between 0 and 1, with higher coefficients indicating higher inequality. For an explanation and further discussion, see Goodman, Johnson and Webb, 1997, pp. 46–50.

5   Blanden and her colleagues examined the relationship between individual earnings and parental income, controlling for other factors that affect earnings, for children born in 1958 and 1970. They found that the association between individual earnings at age sixteen and parental incomes was higher for the cohort born in 1970 than for that born in 1958. Note, however, that this study is looking at *income mobility*, which has to do with the extent to which a child's income performance is affected by parental income. This is not the same thing

as *class mobility*, which is to do with how a child's class position is affected by parental class position.

6 Putnam offers two kinds of evidence for the positive association between social capital and economic equality. Firstly, he shows that trends towards higher income inequality in the USA as a whole began shortly after the recorded decline in social capital. Secondly, he shows that states within the United States with higher measures of social capital tend also to have lower levels of income inequality. He speculates that the relationship between high economic inequality and low social capital may be reciprocal: each contributes to the other, rather than one simply causing the other.

7 To clarify, the claim is not that equality is sufficient for high trust, low crime, low stress and so forth, only that it makes it easier for a society to enjoy them. A further important consideration, which I lack space to develop here, concerns the possible impact of tightening environmental constraints on distributional politics. Might this prompt a renewed sense of shared fate and common purpose which supports egalitarian policies? For an excellent discussion of this issue, see Barry, 2005, pp. 251–73.

8 Blackburn emphasizes the need to democratize control of workers' occupational pension funds and to establish a public pension programme based on collective holdings of commercial assets. Proposals of this kind are significant not only in terms of their possible impact on economic inequality, but also in terms of their potential to address what some see as a fundamental obstacle to political equality: the control that wealthy groups exercise over business investment decisions.

Bibliography

Ackerman, Bruce, *Social Justice in the Liberal State* (New Haven: Yale University Press, 1980).

——, and Alstott, Anne, *The Stakeholder Society* (New Haven: Yale University Press, 1999).

Alesina, Alberto, Glaeser, Edward, and Sacerdote, Bruce, 'Why Doesn't the United States Have a European-Style Welfare State?', *Brookings Papers on Economic Activity* 2 (2001): 187–254.

——, and Glaeser, Edward, *Fighting Poverty in the US and Europe* (Oxford: Oxford University Press, 2004).

Al-Hibri, Azizah Y., 'Is Western Patriarchal Feminism Good for Third World/Minority Women?', Susan M. Okin, *Is Multiculturalism Bad for Women?* (Princeton: Princeton University Press, 1999), pp. 41–6.

Anderson, Elizabeth, 'What is the Point of Equality?', *Ethics* 109 (1999): 287–337.

Aristotle, *The Politics*, trans. Ernest Barker (Oxford: Oxford University Press, 1948).

Arneson, Richard, 'Liberalism, Distributive Subjectivism, and Equal Opportunity for Welfare', *Philosophy and Public Affairs* 19/2 (1990): 158–94.

Ashcraft, Richard, *Revolutionary Politics and Locke's Two Treatises of Government* (Princeton: Princeton University Press, 1986).

Baldwin, James, 'Down at the Cross: Letter from a Region of My Mind', in James Baldwin, *The Fire Next Time* (New York: Dell, 1985 [1962]), pp. 23–141.

Banting, Keith G., 'The Multicultural Welfare State: International

Experience and North American Narratives', *Social Policy and Administration* 39 (2005): 98–115.

Barry, Brian, *The Liberal Theory of Justice* (Oxford: Oxford University Press, 1973).

——, *A Treatise on Social Justice, Volume 1: Theories of Justice* (Berkeley, CA: University of California Press, 1989).

——, *Justice as Impartiality* (Oxford: Oxford University Press, 1995).

——, 'Sustainability and Intergenerational Justice', in Andrew Dobson (ed.), *Fairness and Futurity: Essays on Environmental Sustainability and Social Justice* (Oxford: Oxford University Press, 1999), pp. 93–117.

——, *Culture and Equality* (Cambridge: Polity, 2000).

——, *Why Social Justice Matters* (Cambridge: Polity, 2005).

Beitz, Charles, 'Cosmopolitan Ideals and National Sentiment', *Journal of Philosophy* 80 (1983): 591–600.

——, *Political Equality* (Princeton: Princeton University Press, 1989).

——, *Political Theory and International Relations*, new edition with afterword (Princeton: Princeton University Press, 1999 [1979]).

——, 'Rawls's Law of Peoples', *Ethics* 110 (2000): 669–96.

Bentham, Jeremy, 'Leading Principles of a Constitutional Code', in Bhiku Parekh (ed.), *Bentham's Political Thought* (London: Croom Helm, 1973 [1823]), pp. 195–205.

——, Burns, James H. and Hart, Herbert L. A. (eds), *Introduction to the Principles of Morals and Legislation* (Oxford: Oxford University Press, 1996 [1789]).

Bertram, Christopher, *Rousseau and The Social Contract* (London: Routledge, 2004).

——, 'Global Justice, Moral Development, and Democracy', in Gillian Brock and Harry Brighouse (eds), *The Political Philosophy of Cosmopolitanism* (Cambridge: Cambridge University Press, 2005), pp. 75–91.

Blackburn, Robin, 'The New Collectivism: Pension Reform, Grey Capitalism and Complex Socialism', *New Left Review* 1/233 (1999): 3–65.

——, *Banking on Death – Or, Investing in Life: The History and Future of Pensions* (London: Verso, 2002).

——, *Pensions and the Control of Capitalist Investment* (London: Verso, forthcoming).

Blake, Michael, 'Distributive Justice, State Coercion, and Autonomy', *Philosophy and Public Affairs* 30 (2002): 257–96.

Blanchflower, David, and Oswald, Andrew, 'What Makes an Entrepreneur?', *Journal of Labor Economics* 16 (1998): 26–60.

Blanden, Jo, Goodman, Alissa, Gregg, Paul, and Machin, Stephen, 'Changes in Intergenerational Mobility in Britain', in Miles Corak (ed.), *Generational Income Mobility in North America and Britain* (Cambridge: Cambridge University Press, 2004), pp. 122–46.

Bookchin, Murray, *Post-Scarcity Anarchism* (Berkeley, CA: Ramparts Press, 1971).

——, *Toward an Ecological Society* (Montreal: Black Rose Books, 1980).

——, 'The Communalist Project', *Harbinger: A Journal of Social Ecology* 3 (2003): 20–35.

Bowles, Samuel, 'Introduction', in Bowles, Samuel, Gintis, Herbert, and Osborne Groves, Melissa, *Unequal Chances: Family Background and Economic Success* (New York: Russell Sage Foundation; Princeton: Princeton University Press, 2005), pp. 1–22.

——, Gintis, Herbert, and Osborne Groves, Melissa, *Unequal Chances: Family Background and Economic Success* (New York: Russell Sage Foundation; Princeton: Princeton University Press, 2005).

Brewer, Mike, Goodman, Alissa, Myck, Michal, Shaw, Jonathan, and Shephard, Andrew, *Poverty and Inequality in Britain: 2004* (London: Institute for Fiscal Studies, 2004).

Brighouse, Harry, *Egalitarian Liberalism and Justice in Education* (London: Institute of Education, 2002).

Bryson, Valerie, *Feminist Debates: Issues of Theory and Political Practice* (Basingstoke: Palgrave, 1999).

Burnham, James, *The Managerial Revolution: What is Happening in the World?* (New York: John Day, 1941).

Caney, Simon, 'Review Article: International Distributive Justice', *Political Studies* 49 (2001a): 974–97.

——, 'Cosmopolitan Justice and Equalizing Opportunities', *Metaphilosophy* 32 (2001b): 113–34.

——, 'Entitlements, Obligations, and Distributive Justice: The Global Level', in Daniel A. Bell and Avner de-Shalit (eds), *Forms of Justice: Critical Perspectives on David Miller's Political Philosophy* (Lanham, MD: Rowman and Littlefield, 2003), pp. 287–313.

Carens, Joseph H., *Equality, Moral Incentives, and the Market: An Essay in Utopian Politico-Economic Theory* (Chicago: University of Chicago Press, 1981).

——, 'Rights and Duties in an Egalitarian Society', *Political Theory* 14 (1986): 31–49.

Charles, Nickie, *Gender in Modern Britain* (Oxford: Oxford University Press, 2002).

Che Guevara, Ernesto, 'On the Budgetary Finance System', in David

Deutschmann (ed.), *Che Guevara Reader* (Melbourne: Ocean Press, 1997 [1964]).

Christman, John, 'Self-Ownership, Equality, and the Structure of Property Rights', *Political Theory* 19 (1991): 28–46.

Clayton, Matthew, and Williams, Andrew, 'Some Questions for Egalitarians', in Matthew Clayton and Andrew Williams (eds), *The Ideal of Equality* (London: Macmillan, 2000), pp. 1–20.

Cohen, G. A., 'On the Currency of Egalitarian Justice', *Ethics* 99 (1989): 912–44.

——, 'Incentives, Inequality, and Community', in Grethe B. Peterson (ed.), *The Tanner Lectures on Human Values*, vol. XIII (Salt Lake City: University of Utah Press, 1992), pp. 261–329; and also in Stephen Darwall (ed.), *Equal Freedom: Selected Tanner Lectures on Human Values* (Ann Arbor: Michigan University Press, 1995a), pp. 331–97.

——, *Self-Ownership, Freedom, and Equality* (Cambridge: Cambridge University Press, 1995b).

——, 'Back to Socialist Basics', Appendix: 'On Money and Liberty', in Jane Franklin (ed.), *Equality* (London: Institute for Public Policy Research, 1997), pp. 29–47, specifically pp. 41–3.

——, *If You're an Egalitarian, How Come You're So Rich?* (Cambridge, MA: Harvard University Press, 2000).

Cohen, Joshua, 'Deliberation and Democratic Legitimacy', in James Bohman and William Rehg (eds), *Deliberative Democracy* (Cambridge, MA: MIT Press, 1997a), pp. 67–91.

——, 'The Natural Goodness of Humanity', in Andrews Reath, Barbara Herman, and Christine Korsgaard (eds), *Reclaiming the History of Ethics: Essays for John Rawls* (Cambridge: Cambridge University Press, 1997b), pp. 102–39.

——, 'Taking Men as They Are?', *Philosophy and Public Affairs* 30/4 (2001): 363–86.

——, 'For a Democratic Society', in Samuel Freeman (ed.), *The Cambridge Companion to Rawls* (Cambridge: Cambridge University Press, 2003), pp. 86–138.

——, *A Free Community of Equals: Rousseau on Democracy* (Oxford: Oxford University Press, forthcoming).

——, and Rogers, Joel, 'Secondary Associations and Democratic Governance', in Joshua Cohen and Joel Rogers, with Erik Olin Wright (ed.), *Associations and Democracy* (London: Verso, 1995a), pp. 7–98.

——, and Rogers, Joel, 'Solidarity, Democracy, Association', in Joshua Cohen and Joel Rogers, with Erik Olin Wright (ed.), *Associations and Democracy* (London: Verso, 1995b), pp. 236–67.

——, and Sabel, Charles, 'Directly-Deliberative Polyarchy', *European Law Journal* 3 (1997): 313–42.

——, and Sabel, Charles, 'Extra Republicam, Nulla Justitia?', *Philosophy and Public Affairs* 34/2 (2006): 147–75.

Cole, G. D. H., *Guild Socialism Restated* (London: Allen and Unwin, 1920).

Crompton, Rosemary, *Women and Work in Modern Britain* (Oxford: Oxford University Press, 1997).

Crosland, Anthony, *The Future of Socialism* (London: Jonathan Cape, 1956).

Crouch, Colin, *Post-Democracy* (Cambridge: Polity, 2004).

Dahl, Robert A., 'Decision-Making in a Democracy: The Supreme Court as a National Policy-Maker', *Journal of Public Law* 6/2 (1958): 279–95; also in *Emory Law Journal*, 2001: 563–82.

——, *A Preface to Economic Democracy* (Berkeley and Los Angeles, CA: University of California Press, 1985).

——, *On Democracy* (New Haven, CT: Yale University Press, 1998).

Daniels, Norman, 'Democratic Equality: Rawls's Complex Egalitarianism', in Samuel Freeman (ed.), *The Cambridge Companion to Rawls* (Cambridge: Cambridge University Press, 2003), pp. 241–76.

Dent, Nicholas, *Rousseau: An Introduction to his Psychological, Social and Political Theory* (Oxford: Blackwell, 1988).

——, *Rousseau* (London: Routledge, 2005).

Dryzek, John S., *Deliberative Democracy and Beyond* (Oxford: Oxford University Press, 2000).

Duncan, Graeme, and Lukes, Steven, 'The New Democracy', *Political Studies* 11 (1963): 156–77.

Durkheim, Émile, *Professional Ethics and Civic Morals* (London: Routledge, 1957).

Dworkin, Ronald, 'Why Liberals Should Care About Equality', in Dworkin, *A Matter of Principle* (Cambridge, MA: Harvard University Press, 1985), pp. 205–13.

——, *Sovereign Virtue: The Theory and Practice of Equality* (Cambridge, MA: Harvard University Press, 2000).

——, '*Sovereign Virtue* Revisited', *Ethics* 113 (2002): 106–43.

Erikson, Robert, and Goldthorpe, John, *The Constant Flux: A Study of Class Mobility in Industrial Societies* (Oxford: Oxford University Press, 1992).

Esping-Andersen, Gøsta, 'Inequality of Incomes and Opportunities', in Anthony Giddens and Patrick Diamond (eds), *The New Egalitarianism* (Cambridge: Polity, 2005), pp. 8–38.

Estlund, David, 'Liberalism, Equality and Fraternity in Cohen's Critique of Rawls', *The Journal of Political Philosophy* 6 (1998): 99–112.

Estrin, Saul, and Le Grand, Julian (eds), *Market Socialism* (Oxford: Oxford University Press, 1989).

Fabre, Cécile, 'Global Egalitarianism: An Indefensible Theory of Justice?', in Daniel A. Bell and Avner de-Shalit (eds), *Forms of Justice: Critical Perspectives on David Miller's Political Philosophy* (Lanham, MD: Rowman and Littlefield, 2003), pp. 315–30.

Feinstein, Leon, 'Inequality in the Early Cognitive Development of British Children in the 1970 Cohort', *Economica* 70 (2003): 73–97.

Fishkin, James, *The Voice of the People* (New Haven: Yale University Press, 1995).

Follet, Mary Parker, *The New State: Group Organization the Solution of Popular Government* (University Park, PA: Penn State Press, 1998 [1918]).

Fraser, Nancy, 'From Redistribution to Recognition? Dilemmas of Justice in a "Post-Socialist" Age', *New Left Review* 1/212 (1995): 68–93. Also in Anne Phillips (ed.), *Feminism and Politics* (Oxford: Oxford University Press, 2002), pp. 430–60.

Freeman, Samuel, 'Deliberative Democracy: A Sympathetic Comment', *Philosophy and Public Affairs* 29/4 (2000): 371–418.

——, 'Liberalism and the Accommodation of Group Claims', in Paul Kelly (ed.), *Multiculturalism Reconsidered* (Cambridge: Polity, 2002), pp. 18–30.

Frolich, Norman, and Oppenheimer, Joe A., *Choosing Justice: An Experimental Approach to Ethical Theory* (Berkeley: University of California Press, 1992).

Fukuyama, Francis, *The End of History and the Last Man* (London: Hamish Hamilton, 1992).

Fung, Archon, *Empowered Participation: Reinventing Urban Democracy* (Princeton: Princeton University Press, 2004).

——, and Erik Olin Wright (eds), *Deepening Democracy* (London: Verso, 2003).

Galston, William A., *Liberal Pluralism* (Cambridge: Cambridge University Press, 2002).

——, *The Practice of Liberal Pluralism* (Cambridge: Cambridge University Press, 2004).

George, Henry, *Progress and Poverty* (London: The Hogarth Press, 1966 [1879]).

Gilman, Sander, ' "Barbaric" Rituals?', in Susan M. Okin, *Is Multiculturalism Bad for Women?* (Princeton: Princeton University Press, 1999), pp. 53–8.

Glyn, Andrew, 'Egalitarianism in a Global Economy', *Boston Review*, December 1997/January 1998, available online at <http://www.bostonreview.net/BR22.6/glyn.html>.

——, *Capitalism Unleashed: Finance, Globalization, and Welfare* (Oxford: Oxford University Press, 2006).

Goldthorpe, John, *Social Mobility and Class Structure in Modern Britain* (Oxford: Oxford University Press, 1980).

Goodin, Robert E., *Protecting the Vulnerable* (Chicago: University of Chicago Press, 1986).

——, *Reflective Democracy* (Oxford: Oxford University Press, 2003).

Goodman, Alissa, Johnson, Paul, and Webb, Steven, *Inequality in the UK* (Oxford: Oxford University Press, 1997).

Greenawalt, Kent, 'Five Questions about Religion Judges Are Afraid to Ask', in Nancy Rosenblum (ed.), *Obligations of Citizenship and Demands of Faith* (Princeton: Princeton University Press, 2000), pp. 196–244.

Grofman, Bernard, and Feld, Scott, 'Rousseau's General Will: A Condorcetian Perspective', in Davod Estlund (ed.), *Democracy* (Oxford: Blackwell, 2002 [1988]), pp. 308–19.

Gutmann, Amy, 'Civic Education and Social Diversity', *Ethics* 105 (1995): 557–79.

——, and Thompson, Dennis, *Democracy and Disagreement* (Cambridge, MA: Harvard University Press, 1996).

——, *Why Deliberative Democracy?* (Princeton: Princeton University Press, 2004).

Hall, Peter, and Soskice, David (eds), *Varieties of Capitalism* (Oxford: Oxford University Press, 2001).

Hampsher-Monk, Iain, 'The Political Theory of the Levellers: Putney, Property and Professor MacPherson', *Political Studies* 24 (1976): 397–422.

Hampton, Jean, *Hobbes and the Social Contract Tradition* (Cambridge: Cambridge University Press, 1986).

Harrington, James, J. G. A. Pocock (ed.), *The Commonwealth of Oceana* (Cambridge: Cambridge University Press, 1992 [1656]).

Haveman, Robert, *Starting Even: An Equal Opportunity Program to Combat the Nation's New Poverty* (New York: Simon and Schuster, 1988).

Hayek, Friedrich, *The Road to Serfdom* (Chicago: University of Chicago Press, 1944).

——, *The Constitution of Liberty* (London: Routledge and Kegan Paul, 1960).

Held, David, *Global Covenant: The Social Democratic Alternative to the Washington Consensus* (Cambridge: Polity, 2004).

Hirsch, Fred, *Social Limits to Growth* (London: Routledge and Kegan Paul, 1977).

Hobbes, Thomas, *Leviathan* (Harmondsworth: Penguin, 1985 [1651]).

Hobhouse, Leonard T., *Liberalism*, in James Meadowcroft (ed.), *Liberalism and Other Writings* (Cambridge: Cambridge University Press, 1993 [1911]).

——, *The Labour Movement: Third Edition* (New York: Macmillan, 1912).

Hobsbawm, Eric, 'The Forward March of Labour Halted?', in Martin Jacques and Francis Mulhearn (eds), *The Forward March of Labour Halted?* (London: Verso, 1981), pp. 1–19.

Hoff, Karla, 'Market Failures and the Distribution of Wealth: A Perspective From the Economics of Information', in Samuel Bowles and Herbert Gintis, with Erik Olin Wright (ed.), *Recasting Egalitarianism* (London: Verso, 1998), pp. 332–57.

hooks, bell, *Ain't I a Woman: Black Women and Feminism* (Boston: South End Press, 1981).

——, *Feminist Theory: From Margin to Center: Second Edition* (London: Pluto Press, 2000).

Inland Revenue Statistics 2004 (London: Inland Revenue, 2004).

Jackson, Ben, 'The Uses of Utilitarianism: Social Justice, Welfare Economics and British Socialism, 1931–1948', *History of Political Thought* 24 (2004): 508–35.

Jay, Douglas, *Socialism in the New Society* (London: Longmans, 1962).

Julius, Antony, 'Nagel's Atlas', *Philosophy and Public Affairs* 34/2 (2006): 176–92.

Kant, Immanuel, *On the Common Saying: 'This May be True in Theory, but it does not Apply in Practice'*, trans. H. B. Nisbet in Hans Reiss (ed.), *Kant: Political Writings*, 2nd edn (Cambridge: Cambridge University Press, 1991 [1793]), pp. 61–92.

Kaus, Mickey, *The End of Equality* (New York: Basic Books, 1992).

Keister, Lisa A., *Wealth in America: Trends in Wealth Inequality* (Cambridge: Cambridge University Press, 2000).

Kenworthy, Lane, *Egalitarian Capitalism: Jobs, Incomes, and Growth in Affluent Societies* (New York: Russell Sage Foundation, 2004).

King, Loren, 'The Federal Structure of a Republic of Reasons', *Political Theory* 33 (2005): 629–53.

Kingsnorth, Paul, *One No, Many Yeses* (New York: The Free Press, 2003).

Kramer, Larry D., *The People Themselves: Popular Constitutionalism and Judicial Review* (Oxford: Oxford University Press, 2004).

Kropotkin, Peter, *Modern Science and Anarchism*, in Roger N. Baldwin (ed.), *Kropotkin's Revolutionary Pamphlets* (New York: Dover, 1970 [1913]), pp. 146–94.

Kuper, Andrew, 'Rawlsian Global Justice: Beyond the Law of Peoples to a Cosmopolitan Law of Persons', *Political Theory* 28 (2000): 640–74.

Kymlicka, Will, *Liberalism, Community and Culture* (Oxford: Oxford University Press, 1989).

——, *Multicultural Citizenship* (Oxford: Oxford University Press, 1995).

——, *Contemporary Political Philosophy: An Introduction*, 2nd edn (Oxford: Oxford University Press, 2000).

Lareau, Annette, *Unequal Childhoods: Class, Race, and Family Life* (Berkeley, CA: University of California Press, 2003).

Locke, John, Peter Laslett (ed.), *Two Treatises of Government* (Cambridge: Cambridge University Press, 1960 [1689]).

Mabey, Richard, 'Introduction: Not on Speaking Terms', in Richard Mabey (ed.), *Class: A Symposium* (London: Anthony Blond, 1966), pp. 7–17.

Macchiavelli, Niccolò, *The Discourses* (Harmondsworth: Penguin, 1970 [1531]).

McKay, Stephen, and Kempson, Elaine, *Savings and Life Events*, DWP Report 94 (London: Department of Work and Pensions, 2003).

MacPherson, C. B., *The Political Theory of Possessive Individualism* (Oxford: Oxford University Press, 1962).

Marshall, Gordon, and Swift, Adam, 'Meritocratic Equality of Opportunity: Economic Efficiency, Social Justice, or Both?', *Policy Studies* 18 (1997): 35–48.

——, ——, and Roberts, Stephen, *Against the Odds? Social Class and Social Justice in Industrial Societies* (Oxford: Oxford University Press, 1997).

Marshall, T. H., 'Citizenship and Social Class', in Marshall, *Citizenship and Social Class* (Cambridge: Cambridge University Press, 1950), pp. 1–85.

Marx Karl, *The Critique of the Gotha Programme*, excerpted in David McLellan (ed.), *Karl Marx: Selected Writings* (Oxford: Oxford University Press, 1977 [1875]), pp. 564–70.

——, *Capital: Volume 1*, trans. Ernst Mandel (Harmonsworth: Penguin, 1990 [1865]).

——, and Engels, Friedrich, *The Communist Manifesto* (Harmondsworth: Penguin, 2002 [1848]).

Mead, Lawrence, *The New Politics of Poverty: The Nonworking Poor in America* (New York: Basic Books, 1992).

Meade, James, *Efficiency, Equality, and the Ownership of Property* (London: Allen and Unwin, 1964).

——, *Agathatopia: The Economics of Partnership* (Aberdeen: University of Aberdeen Press, 1989).

Mill, James, *Essay on Government*, in Jack Lively and John Ress (eds), *Utilitarian Logic and Politics* (Oxford: Oxford University Press, 1978 [1824/25]), pp. 53–95.

Mill, John Stuart, *On Liberty* (Harmondsworth: Penguin, 1985 [1859]).

——, *On the Subjection of Women* in Stefan Collini (ed.), *On Liberty and Other Writings* (Cambridge: Cambridge University Press, 1989 [1869]), pp. 117–217.

——, *Utilitarianism*, in John Stuart Mill, Geraint Williams (ed.), *Utilitarianism, On Liberty, Considerations on Representative Government, Remarks on Bentham's Philosophy* (London: Dent, 1993a [1861]), pp. 1–67.

——, *Considerations on Representative Government*, in John Stuart Mill, Geraint Williams (ed.), *Utilitarianism, On Liberty, Considerations on Representative Government, Remarks on Bentham's Philosophy* (London: Dent, 1993b [1861]), pp. 187–428.

Miller, David, 'Why Markets?', in Saul Estrin and Julian Le Grand (eds), *Market Socialism* (Oxford: Oxford University Press, 1989a), pp. 25–49.

——, *Market, State, and Community: The Theoretical Foundations of Market Socialism* (Oxford: Oxford University Press, 1989b).

——, 'Complex Equality', in David Miller and Michael Walzer (eds), *Pluralism, Justice, and Equality* (Oxford: Oxford University Press, 1994), pp. 197–225.

——, 'The Limits of Cosmopolitan Justice', in David R. Mapel and Terry Nardin (eds), *International Society: Diverse Ethical Perspectives* (Princeton: Princeton University Press, 1998), pp. 164–81.

——, *Principles of Social Justice* (Cambridge, MA: Harvard University Press, 2000a).

——, *Citizenship and National Identity* (Cambridge: Polity, 2000b).

Milton, John, *The Tenure of Kings and Magistrates*, in Malcolm W. Wallace (ed.), *Milton's Prose* (London: Oxford University Press, 1925 [1650]), pp. 325–71.

Minow, Martha, *Making All the Difference: Inclusion, Exclusion, and American Law* (Ithaca, NY: Cornell University Press, 1990).

Modood, Tariq, Berthoud, Richard, Lakey, Jane, Nazroo, James, Smith, Patten, Virdee, Satnam, and Beishon, Sharon, *Ethnic Minorities in Britain: Diversity and Disadvantage* (London: Policy Studies Institute, 1997).

Moon, J. Donald, 'Review of Joseph Carens's *Equality, Moral Incentives, and the Market*', *Ethics* 94 (1983): 146–50.

Musgrave, Richard, 'Maximin, Uncertainty, and the Leisure Trade-Off', *Quarterly Journal of Economics* 88 (1974): 625–32.

Nagel, Thomas, 'Equality', in Thomas Nagel, *Mortal Questions* (Cambridge: Cambridge University Press, 1979), pp. 106–27.

——, *Equality and Partiality* (Oxford: Oxford University Press, 1991).

——, 'The Problem of Global Justice', *Philosophy and Public Affairs* 33/2 (2005): 113–47.

Nelson, Eric, *The Greek Tradition in Republican Thought* (Cambridge: Cambridge University Press, 2004).

Nissan, David, and Le Grand, Julian, *A Capital Start: Start-up Grants for Young People* (London: Fabian Society, 2000).

Nozick, Robert, *Anarchy, State, and Utopia* (Oxford: Blackwell, 1974).

Nussbaum, Martha C., 'Aristotelian Social Democracy', in R. Bruce Douglas, Gerald M. Mara and Henry S. Richardson (eds), *Liberalism and the Good* (New York: Routledge, 1990), pp. 203–52.

——, 'Human Functioning and Social Justice: In Defense of Aristotelian Essentialism', *Political Theory* 20 (1992): 202–46.

——, 'A Plea for Difficulty', in Susan M. Okin, *Is Multiculturalism Bad for Women?* (Princeton: Princeton University Press, 1999), pp. 105–14.

——, *Women and Human Development: The Capabilities Approach* (Cambridge: Cambridge University Press, 2000).

Okin, Susan Moller, *Women in Western Political Thought* (Princeton: Princeton University Press, 1979).

——, *Justice, Gender, and the Family* (New York: Basic Books, 1989).

——, *Is Multiculturalism Bad for Women?*, with Joshua Cohen, Matthew Howard, and Martha C. Nussbaum (eds) (Princeton: Princeton University Press, 1999).

Orwell, George, *Homage to Catalonia* (Harmondsworth: Penguin, 1989 [1938]).

——, *Nineteen Eighty-Four* (Harmondsworth: Penguin, 2004 [1949]).

Paine, Thomas, *The Rights of Man: Part One*, in Michael Foot and Isaac Kramnick (eds), *The Thomas Paine Reader* (Harmondsworth: Penguin, 1987 [1791]), pp. 201–62.

——, *Agrarian Justice*, in Michael Foot and Isaac Kramnick (eds), *The Thomas Paine Reader* (Harmondsworth: Penguin, 1987 [1797]), pp. 471–89.

Pannekoek, Anton, Robert F. Barsky (ed.), *Workers' Councils* (New York: AK Press, 2002 [1948]).

Parekh, Bhiku, 'Equality in a Multicultural Society', in Jane Franklin (ed.), *Equality* (London: Institute for Public Policy Research, 1997).

——, 'A Varied Moral World', in Susan M. Okin, *Is Multiculturalism Bad for Women?* (Princeton: Princeton University Press, 1999), pp. 69–75.

——, *Rethinking Multiculturalism* (Basingstoke: Palgrave, 2000).

Parfit, Derek, 'Equality or Priority?', in Matthew Clayton and

Andrew Williams (eds), *The Ideal of Equality* (London: Macmillan, 2000), pp. 81–125.

Pateman, Carole, *Participation and Democratic Theory* (Oxford: Oxford University Press, 1970).

——, *The Sexual Contract* (Cambridge: Polity, 1988).

Paxton, Will, 'The Asset-Effect: An Overview', in John Bynner and Will Paxton, *The Asset-Effect* (London: Institute for Public Policy Research, 2001).

——, and Dixon, Mike, 'The State of the Nation: An Audit of Social Injustice in the UK', in Nick Pearce and Will Paxton (eds), *Social Justice: Building a Fairer Britain* (London: Politico's, 2005), pp. 21–61.

——, and Stuart White with Dominic Maxwell (eds), *The Citizen's Stake: Exploring the Future of Universal Asset Policies* (Bristol: Policy Press, 2006).

Pearce, Nick, 'Diversity Versus Solidarity: A New Progressive Dilemma', *Renewal* 12/3 (2004): 79–87.

Pettit, Philip, *Republicanism: A Theory of Freedom and Government* (Oxford: Oxford University Press, 1997).

Phillips, Anne, *The Politics of Presence* (Oxford: Oxford University Press, 1995).

Plato, *The Apology*, trans. G. M. A. Grube, in Grube (ed.), *Five Dialogues* (Indianopolis, IN: Hackett, 1981).

——, *Republic*, trans. G. M. A. Grube and C. D. C. Reeve (Indianopolis, IN: Hackett, 1992 [380 BCE]).

——, *Protagoras*, trans. C. C. W. Taylor (Oxford: Oxford University Press, 1996).

——, *Gorgias*, trans. Walter Hamilton and Chris Emlyn-Jones (Harmondsworth: Penguin, 2004).

——, *The Laws*, trans. Trevor J. Saunders (Harmondsworth: Penguin, 2004).

Pogge, Thomas, *Realizing Rawls* (Ithaca, NY: Cornell University Press, 1989).

——, 'An Egalitarian Law of Peoples', *Philosophy and Public Affairs* 23 (1994): 195–224.

——, 'On the Site of Distributive Justice: Reflections on Cohen and Murphy', *Philosophy and Public Affairs* 29/2 (2000): 137–69.

——, *World Poverty and Human Rights* (Cambridge: Polity, 2002).

Polybius, *The Rise of the Roman Empire*, trans. Ian Scott-Kilvert (Harmondsworth: Penguin, 1979).

Przeworski, Adam, 'Minimalist Conception of Democracy: A Defense', in Ian Shapiro and Casiano Hacker-Cordón (eds), *Democracy's Value* (Cambridge: Cambridge University Press, 1999), pp. 23–55.

Putnam, Robert D., *Bowling Alone: The Collapse and Revival of American Community* (New York: Simon and Schuster, 2000).

Rathbone, Eleanor, *The Disinherited Family: A Plea For the Endowment of the Family* (London: Edward Arnold, 1924).

Rawls, John, *A Theory of Justice: Revised Edition* (Cambridge, MA: Harvard University Press, 1999a [1971]).

——, *Political Liberalism* (New York: Columbia University Press, 1993).

——, *The Law of Peoples* (Cambridge, MA: Harvard University Press, 1999b).

——, *Justice as Fairness: A Restatement* (Cambridge, MA: Harvard University Press, 2001).

Raz, Joseph, *The Morality of Freedom* (Oxford: Oxford University Press, 1986).

Rhode, Deborah, 'The Politics of Paradigms: Gender Difference and Gender Disadvantage', in Anne Phillips (ed.), *Feminism and Politics* (Oxford: Oxford University Press, 1998 [1992]), pp. 344–62.

Roberts, Ken, *Class in Modern Britain* (Basingstoke: Palgrave, 2001).

Roemer, John, *A Future for Socialism* (Cambridge, MA: Harvard University Press, 1994).

Rousseau, Jean-Jacques, translated by Maurice Cranston, *A Discourse on Inequality* (Harmondsworth: Penguin, 1984 [1755]).

——, translated by Christopher Betts, *The Social Contract* (Oxford: Oxford University Press, 1994 [1762]).

Rowlingson, Karen, and McKay, Stephen, *Attitudes to Inheritance in Britain* (York: Joseph Rowntree Foundation, 2005).

Ryan, Alan, 'Locke and the Dictatorship of the Bourgeoisie', *Political Studies* 13 (1965): 219–30.

Satz, Debra, 'Inequality of What and Among Whom?', paper delivered at the Annual Meeting of the American Political Science Association, San Francisco, September 1996.

Saunders, Peter, 'Might Britain Be a Meritocracy?', *Sociology* 29 (1995): 23–41.

Savage, Mike, and Egerton, Muriel, 'Social Mobility, Individual Ability and the Inheritance of Class Inequality', *Sociology* 31 (1997): 645–72.

Scanlon, Thomas, *What We Owe to Each Other* (Cambridge, MA: Harvard University Press, 1999).

——, 'The Diversity of Objections to Inequality', in Thomas Scanlon, *The Difficulty of Tolerance* (Cambridge: Cambridge University Press, 2003), pp. 202–18.

Scheffler, Samuel, 'Responsibility, Reactive Attitudes, and Liberalism in Philosophy and Politics', *Philosophy and Public Affairs* 21/4 (1992): 299–323.

——, 'What is Egalitarianism?', *Philosophy and Public Affairs* 31/1 (2003): 5–39.

Sen, Amartya, *Inequality Reexamined* (Oxford: Oxford University Press, 1992).

——, *Development as Freedom* (Oxford: Oxford University Press, 1999).

Sharp, Andrew (ed.), *The English Levellers* (Cambridge: Cambridge University Press, 1998).

Shavit, Yossi, and Bossfeld, Hans-Peter, *Persistent Inequality: Changing Educational Attainment in Thirteen Countries* (Boulder, CO: Westview Press, 1993).

Shaw, George Bernard, 'The Basis of Socialism: Economic', in George Bernard Shaw (ed.), *Fabian Essays in Socialism* (Boston: The Ball Publishing Company, 1909 [1889]), pp. 1–25.

——, *The Intelligent Woman's Guide to Socialism, Capitalism, Sovietism and Fascism* (Harmondsworth: Penguin, 1937).

Singer, Peter, *Animal Liberation: Second Edition* (New York: New York Review of Books, 1990 [1975]).

Skinner, Quentin, *Liberty Before Liberalism* (Cambridge: Cambridge University Press, 1998).

Smith, Graham, and Wales, Corinne, 'Citizens' Juries and Deliberative Democracy', *Political Studies* 48 (2000): 51–65.

Smith, Rogers M., ' "Equal Treatment"? A Liberal Separationist View', in Stephen V. Monsma and J. Christopher Soper (eds), *Equal Treatment of Religion in a Pluralist Society* (Grand Rapids, Michigan: Eerdmans, 1998), pp. 179–99.

Sowell, Thomas, *Markets and Minorities* (Oxford: Blackwell, 1981).

Spelman, Elizabeth, *Inessential Woman: Problems of Exclusion in Feminist Thought* (Boston: Beacon Press, 1988).

Spencer, Herbert, *Social Statics: First Edition* (New York: Appleton and Company, 1872 [1850]).

Sunstein, Cass, 'Why Markets Won't Stop Discrimination', *Social Philosophy and Policy* 8 (1991): 22–37.

Swift, Adam, *Political Philosophy: A Beginners' Guide for Students and Politicians* (Cambridge: Polity, 2001).

——, 'Seizing the Opportunity: The Influence of Preferences and Aspirations on Social Immobility', *New Economy* 10 (2003): 208–12.

——, 'Would Perfect Mobility be Perfect?', *European Sociological Review* 20/1 (2004): 1–11.

Tawney, R. H., *The Acquisitive Society* (New York: Harcourt Brace Jovanovich, 1948 [1920]).

——, *Equality* (London: Allen and Unwin, 1964 [1931]).

Taylor, Charles, 'The Politics of Recognition', in Amy Gutmann (ed.), *Multiculturalism and the 'Politics of Recognition'* (Princeton: Princeton University Press, 1992), pp. 25–73.

Taylor-Gooby, Peter, 'Is the Future American? Or, Can Left Politics Preserve European Welfare States from Erosion through Growing 'Racial' Diversity?', *Journal of Social Policy* 34 (2005): 661–72.

Temkin, Larry, 'Equality, Priority, and the Levelling Down Objection', in Matthew Clayton and Andrew Williams (eds), *The Ideal of Equality* (London: Macmillan, 2000), pp. 126–61.

Tocqueville, Alexis de, *Democracy in America*, Vols 1 and 2 (New York: Vintage, 1990 [1835; 1840]).

Tully, James, *Strange Multiplicity* (Cambridge: Cambridge University Press, 1995).

Tushnet, Mark, 'Democracy versus Judicial Review: Is It Time to Amend the Constitution?', *Dissent*, Spring 2005, available on-line at: <http://www.dissentmagazine.org/menutest/articles/sp05/tushnet.htm>.

United Nations Development Programme, *Human Development Report 1999* (New York: Oxford University Press, 1999).

van der Veen, Robert, 'Equality of Talent Resources: Procedures or Outcomes?', *Ethics* 113 (2002): 55–82.

——, 'Basic Income Versus Wage Subsidies: Competing Instruments in an Optimal Tax Model with a Maximin Objective', *Economics and Philosophy* 20 (2004): 147–83.

van Donselaar, Gijs, *The Benefit of Another's Pains* (Amsterdam: University of Amsterdam, 1997).

Van Parijs, Philippe, *Real Freedom for All: What (if Anything) Can Justify Capitalism?* (Oxford: Oxford University Press, 1995).

——, 'The Disfranchisement of the Elderly, and Other Attempts to Secure Intergenerational Justice', *Philosophy and Public Affairs* 27/4 (1998): 292–333.

——, 'Difference Principles', in Samuel Freeman (ed.), *The Cambridge Companion to Rawls* (Cambridge: Cambridge University Press, 2003), pp. 200–40.

Waldron, Jeremy, 'Theoretical Foundations of Liberalism', in Jeremy Waldron, *Liberal Rights* (Cambridge: Cambridge University Press, 1993a), pp. 35–62.

——, 'Homelessness and the Issue of Freedom', in Jeremy Waldron, *Liberal Rights* (Cambridge: Cambridge University Press, 1993b), pp. 309–38.

——, 'John Rawls and the Social Minimum', in Jeremy Waldron, *Liberal Rights* (Cambridge: Cambridge University Press, 1993c), pp. 250–70.

——, 'Minority Cultures and the Cosmopolitan Alternative', in Will Kymlicka (ed.), *The Rights of Minority Cultures* (Oxford: Oxford University Press, 1995), pp. 93–119.

——, 'The Constitutional Conception of Democracy', in David Estlund (ed.), *Democracy* (Oxford: Blackwell, 2002), pp. 51–83.

——, 'On Judicial Review', *Dissent*, Summer 2005, available online at: <http://www.dissentmagazine.org/menutest/articles/su05/waldron.htm>.

Wells, H. G., *The Open Conspiracy: Blue Prints for a World Revolution* (London: Victor Gollancz, 1928).

White, Stuart, 'Freedom of Association and the Right to Exclude', *Journal of Political Philosophy* 5/4 (1997): 373–91.

——, 'Trade Unionism in a Liberal State,' in Amy Gutmann (ed.), *Freedom of Association* (Princeton: Princeton University Press, 1998), pp. 330–54.

——, 'The Egalitarian Earnings Subsidy Scheme', *British Journal of Political Science* 29/4 (1999): 601–22.

Wilkinson, Martin, *Freedom, Efficiency and Equality* (Basingstoke: Macmillan, 2000).

Wilkinson, Richard G., *The Impact of Inequality: How to Make Sick Societies Healthier* (London: Routledge, 2005).

Williams, Andrew, 'Incentives, Inequality, and Publicity', *Philosophy and Public Affairs* 27/3 (1998): 97–122.

——, 'Dworkin on Capability', *Ethics* 113 (2002): 23–39.

Williams, Bernard, 'The Idea of Equality', in Bernard Williams, *Problems of the Self* (Cambridge: Cambridge University Press, 1973), pp. 230–49.

Wissenburg, Marcel, *Green Liberalism: The Free and the Green Society* (London: University College of London Press, 1998).

Wolff, Jonathan, *Robert Nozick: Property, Justice and the Minimal State* (Cambridge: Polity, 1991).

——, 'Fairness, Respect, and the Egalitarian Ethos', *Philosophy and Public Affairs* 27/2 (1998): 97–122.

Wollstonecraft, Mary, *A Vindication of the Rights of Woman*, in Sylvana Tomaselli (ed.), *A Vindication of the Rights of Men and A Vindication of the Rights of Woman* (Cambridge: Cambridge University Press, 1995 [1792]).

Woodin, Michael, and Lucas, Caroline, *Green Alternatives To Globalization: A Manifesto* (London: Pluto, 2004).

Woodruff, Paul, *First Democracy: The Challenge of an Ancient Idea* (Oxford: Oxford University Press, 2005).

Wright, Erik Olin, *Class Counts: Comparative Studies in Class Analysis* (Cambridge: Cambridge University Press, 1997).

Young, Iris Marion, 'Polity and Group Difference: A Critique of the Ideal of Universal Citizenship', *Ethics* 99 (1989): 250–77.

——, *Justice and the Politics of Difference* (Princeton: Princeton University Press, 1990).

Young, Michael, *The Rise of the Meritocracy* (London: Thames and Hudson, 1958).

Index

CPSIA information can be obtained
at www.ICGtesting.com
Printed in the USA
BVHW040213290921
617720BV00010B/90